Dispelling the Binary

Dispelling the Binary

lucid dawn

Contents

~ { V }

~ { *VII* }

Readers Celebrate Dispelling the Binary

"Dispelling the Binary is one timely and powerful book! We often hear the phrase 'non-duality' as it applies to spiritual thinking, but this book gives us real, practical ways to refute the extremes that have harmed so many of us and bring the glory of inclusivity alive in our day-to-day lives and relationships.

In the same way that our precious lives are beautifully dynamic and complex, this book's scope of inquiry is wide and carries us through non - binary pathways including psychological understanding, earth based, yogic and buddhist philosophies, artistic expression, history and cultural understanding of gender fluidity, sex, sexual expression, living systems of interconnectedness, and so much more. It includes exercises and inquiries to unpack inherited traumas and bring the exploration of the book's themes into our somatic awareness. It is a tender, loving reclamation of our human nuance and connection to the web of life.

The whole world is alive with beauty beyond the binary, and lucid is your sparkling guide to the place where healing and magic happen!"

- **Suzanne Sterling, Founder: Voice of Change and Art of Ritual, Cofounder: Off the Mat, Into the World, and Auricle Collective.** SuzanneSterling.com

"An approachable book of magnificent scope. *Dispelling the Binary* is a fun-to-read, practical handbook to understand and reshape our binary thinking. Like her name, lucid's book is clear and enlightening. This book addresses the very important work our generation is undertaking on gender. And it's about *so much more* than gender! Drawing on spiritual lineages including yoga, tantra, and alchemy, lucid invites the reader to deconstruct the spell of binary thinking in service to wholeness and unity. lucid's transmission is embodied, humble, and brilliant. *Dispelling the Binary* is a valuable resource for everyone, including folx just beginning their journey to understand sex and gender, and experienced sex-educators like myself. This book is a gem!"

- Matt Sturm, author of The Organic Masculine

"Dispelling the Binary guides readers through a series of thoughtful, clearly explained practices designed to explore the reality of our nonbinary existence. This book is perfect for those seeking a deeper, personal understanding of the complexities underlying our culture. While gender is a starting point, it opens the door to how nonbinary thinking can broaden our understanding of ourselves and the world around us. In these divided times, this practical guide is a vital tool for healing culture."

- Polly Superstar, author, artist, performer, and provocateur. PollySuperstar.com

"Lucid Dawn is the most courageous person I know. In reading this book, I have discovered that she is also one of the wisest. I was struck by the compassionate and accessible synthesis of so many diverse healing schools and wisdom traditions. This book is also written to help us step out of our comfort zones or defensive postures, past our fears or uncertainties, and learn different ways of language and being with respect to the prevailing binary conventions on gender. This magnificent book is a tool for both learning and healing, for us as individuals and also as a society."

- Peter Schurman, One Global Democracy

"Profoundly needed in these times of rapid change, lucid has created a refreshingly practical workbook for expanding beyond limiting beliefs into the rapture of a nuanced life. Potent for the reader and for self-development leaders, I will certainly be weaving the simple yet powerful activities outlined in this book to guide others in our future Emotional Intelligence Trainings.

- Cristina Star, founder, TRU Education & Cosmic Citizen Trainings

"What a fantastic book that could not be more timely or important. Lucid Dawn invites us into a multidimensional inquiry that is a testament to the depths of her path and dedication to supporting others. This work needs to be done in our communities, and the book provides maps, tools, and structure for doing so. I hope that this vital book gets into many hands and reaches many hearts."

 - **Pamela Rosin, MFT, Founder of ReParentive® Therapy**

"In *Dispelling the Binary*, lucid compiles 30 years of rebirthing-practice and 20+ years of dedicated teaching of trauma-informed yoga and Tantrik lineages in an easy-to-read volume that is part memoir, part reference book, practice manual and workbook, to help all of us dispel the crushing binaries pressed upon us by outside forces to segregate our parts as a means of control.

Our true nature is nonbinary and free. All of us. From the most privileged to the most marginalized. In a book that reaches beyond self-help to discuss how false binaries seek to control us systemically through the false gender binary, the invented racial binary, and all other forms of systemic oppression, lucid offers practical steps, beginning in each of our bodies, to dissolve the the externally-imposed walls in our physical and energetic bodies to support us in coming back to our true nature. We are unbridled, free, blissfully nonbinary in every way. Open this book if you dare to reclaim your true nature."

 - **Arielle Tonkin, Artivist, Interfaith Social Justice Educator, Yogini**

Dedication

I dedicate this work to my love, Jess Sifuentes Chubb, FNP, aka Jess Please (she/they). She was an earth angel of care, compassion, and unconditional love who gave tirelessly to those in deepest need. Jess taught me so much about dispelling my binary conditioning even though I was already years into this study and practice. They supported me in creating the workshop that was the seed of this book, and they were its first editor. She left this earthly plane while we were still editing to become a sky angel, 11 days after turning 45, and 2 months after a stage 4 cancer diagnosis. Many of us were devastated by her sudden departure from embodied life and have had to come to terms with the fact that we never know how long anyone has to be here.

Jess, may this work honor your memory and carry forth the permission and power you brought to the world. May it make life easier for those who come after you. May your memory and legacy live on to inspire and uplift the hearts of many. May all beings be free to love and express, dress, use public restrooms, play sports and dance as their truth inspires, free of shame and harm.

I love you infinitely, Jess. I feel you guiding my hand as I complete this work. Thank you for all of the love and blessings that you continue to bestow...

Introduction

"*Purno'ham vimarsa*" - The real "I" encompasses everything

Once upon a time I was confused about why I had multiple voices in my head with conflicting stories about who I was. How could I be a sissy and a tomboy, have multi-colored skin and family, yet be called white, be called both smarty pants and stupid, be a slut and a prude, shy and a big mouth, powerful and weak, feel broken and healed and everything in between, all at once!? What is wrong with me!? Does everyone else know who they are except me? I wondered.

And then,
An emotional breakdown
Caused a breakthrough
(as they do)
& this happened again & again
& over time
I came to fully realize
I get to be ALL OF IT!
Because I can be
Because I AM (and so are you)

NOW.

We live in a time of turning, a rapidly evolving time. All of us have been impacted by binary thinking and divisive rhetoric. It is becoming more obvious that living in denial, separation, and othering is painful and unsustainable. We are being urged by necessity to expand our worldview. It is time to envision a future where all beings thrive in more inclusive and caring social, economic, and ecological structures. Without this, neither we nor our planet can truly thrive. Interdependence is at the core of life here on Earth.

This book addresses how binary thinking and language affect us all. Through self-reflective practices and invitations to community dialogue we will explore many ways that binary thinking has influenced our world while leaning into a significant focus on gender. The goal is to expand awareness of the effects of words and worldviews on our relationships. We will look at binary thinking and ways of dispelling it while healing into wholeness through the lenses of multiple modalities. With each modality's wisdom and inspiration, you can reflect on your own experiences and insights. The references and exercises ahead are a starting point for self-discovery. Through this transformative process, you will become more compassionate and conscientiously connected to your Self and others.

Who This Work Is For

The content of this book is vital to those who are in service to others: teachers, leaders, bosses, activists, artists, parents, and healers. For those ready to do the inner work, we can empower ourselves and others through being open-minded and radically inclusive of the movements occurring in our inner and outer worlds. We can do this through mindfulness, meditation, psychology, philosophy, embodied practices, spirituality, and ritual.

The content of this book encourages awakening to our already-wholeness and our inextricable interconnectedness with one another, earth, and spirit. It might help someone you love feel clearer about who they are and their place in this world. It can also help you love and understand someone challenging to you right now—including yourself!

This content was first created for a 'conscious community' festival workshop once I realized that many of those folx were not as conscious of some things as they wanted to be. Aliveness is about growth and connection. It is a natural impulse for humans to connect. All beings have good hearts, even beneath bad behavior and willful ignorance. Most people want to be inclusive but many do not know how to engage with the unfamiliar. If there is a lack of information or exposure to certain groups of people then xenophobia or just sheer ignorance can end up causing pain and division instead of connection.

This book is offered in service to healing the binary thinking that makes people feel othered, separate, divided, or unworthy of love and belonging. This thinking and the behavior it breeds causes violence on every level of being. **If you have ever been unsure how to connect or engage with others or your whole Self, this work is for you.** It speaks to those on a path of self-inquiry, healing, truth-seeking, and social justice. As the world changes, familiar foundations become shaky, and what was once accepted may not be so anymore. As our youth expand their worldviews and self-expression, we must be present and prepared to support them in thriving. We can do this best by staying open-minded, learning, and living into our fullness.

Gathered here is a collection of timeless spiritual wisdom, therapeutic views, personal stories, historical perspectives, and proposed inquiries to help you find your truth. **I do not propose to tell you how to think, I open many windows to views that can bring more inspiration, permission, and love into your life.** May we all have the resources we need to grow healthy selves, families, and communities that support each other in thriving.

The Journey Ahead

- **Expand your awareness:** Become more aware of binary limitations and their impact on your consciousness.

- **Connect with your experience:** Connect to and witness the binary thinking, speech habits, and experiences of yourself and others.
- **Open to the fullness of complexity:** Learn more about yourself and community using practices and exercises that can be done alone or with others.
- **Heal division:** This work will help you thoughtfully engage with people who are different from you and your previous experiences of the world.
- **Deepen your understanding:** Explore gender, sex, and sexuality, as well as other areas where binary constructs have shaped your experience.
- **Engage in self-investigation:** Thoughtfully and compassionately examine your behavior with reflective exercises focusing on your experience.
- **Recognize your resistance:** Discover how you resist and cut out parts of yourself and those with whom you share the world. When we suffer division, it isn't only as individuals but as a whole.

FACTS:

Binary thinking perpetuates harm in many ways, from violence to chronic illness and systemic inequity. For example, a study by the American Psychological Association (APA) found that individuals forced to conform to traditional gender roles are more likely to experience anxiety, depression, and low self-esteem. Also, binary racial constructs continue to contribute to systemic inequality. As per Federal Reserve statistics for 2019 in the United States, Black households have a median wealth of $24,100 compared to $188,200 for White households. These facts are just a couple of many that demonstrate how deeply embedded binary constructs harm individuals and societies.

Container Setting

The content of this book is designed to be a workshop/ritual healing and growth process. We honor this space by acknowledging our time/space, all that supports us, and by creating agreements for harmony within ourselves and with those whom we are working with.

Agreements:

- **Consent:** You can consent or decline to participate in any exercise. This journey is yours. Choose what feels right.
- **Spiritual authority:** You are your own guide. Receive what speaks to you and ignore what does not.
- **Lean into discomfort:** This work can be challenging. Courage and vulnerability are valuable in this space.
- **Visibility:** If any part of you feels unseen, acknowledge it. All parts of you are welcome to be an active part of this dialogue.
- **Assume best intentions:** I want to hear when my impact differs from my intention. I welcome feedback and encourage you to reach out to me online.

- **Confidentiality:** If you are working through this book with others, agree that personal stories will not be shared outside the group.

Land Acknowledgment

When I first presented this work, I was on the land of the Wappo and Miwok tribes. I primarily wrote the work on the unceded homeland of the Chochenyo Muwekma Ohlone people in what is commonly known as Oakland, CA.

I do not know the gender variants of these tribes, as land and gender have both been colonized. Indigenous people worldwide have fought to preserve their ancestral lands, languages, and cultures. Much has been lost, and much we work to reclaim. This acknowledgment is a tiny part of that. Whose land are you on? We must know our past to move forward with integrity.

Hail and honor to the original people of the land we inhabit. May you thrive, and may we give back where we can.

Honor Teachers, Lineages, & Activist Ancestors

As you begin, I invite you to take a moment to honor those who have been guides on your path. For me, these have been my step-sibling, Vic, my drag family in NYC, my Reclaiming Community, especially Starhawk and Suzanne Sterling, my teacher Hareesh Wallis, his teacher Gurumayi and her writings, and those who preceded them in Non-Dual Tantrik Saivism lineages. I extend deep gratitude to my love Jess for their incisive thinking, keen listening, and support of my being vigilant about how binary conditioning shows up in me. Thank you to my brilliant students, teachers, and friends, Jane Arc and turtle woman, for their generous support and input to this book. Thank you to my awesome child, Ola'i Manu Mele and their whole generation, who have grown to naturally rebel against many of the painful, confusing, and useless binaries that they had set before them. We are all growing up together in this way.

I also extend heartfelt thanks to all of the activist ancestors and transcestors whose lives and work make our current freedoms and understanding of who we are possible. Here are just a few; Marsha P. Johnson, Silvia Rivera, Harvey Milk, Lucy Hicks Anderson, Walt Whitman, Sappho, Dr. Margaret Chung, Amelio Robles Avila, Bayard Rustin, James Baldwin, Billy Tipton.. and did you know that Shakespeare wrote 126 love poems to a man? So many queer activist ancestors have gone unrecognized. Let us share a breath to honor those beings as well...

Reflection Prompts:

Start your journey by pausing to acknowledge and honor the land you are on and the land's original people.

Now reflect:

- Who has guided you on your path?
- What teachers or lineages have influenced you?
- Have any queer, visionary, and/or activist ancestors inspired you?

{ 1 }

Duality & Unity

Binary conditioning runs deep. We have all suffered binary identity assignments: girl/boy, good/bad, smart/stupid, black/white, right/wrong, left/right, beautiful/ugly, virgin/whore, sacred/profane, masculine/feminine, in/out, too much/not enough. These labels constrain identity and self-expression. They do not acknowledge the spectrum of source, experience, and possibilities that we all are and can be. We are all constellations of being, "multi-racial" (yet all of the human race), masculine and feminine, introverted extroverts, informed in some areas while ignorant in others, open-minded yet conservative on different topics. Often, these identifiers will vary and be influenced by our life cycles, ages, and the company we are in.

Even as I explain binary conditioning it afflicts me. I have found myself contradicting what I am actually trying to express, as in; "I just want this to be 'good.'" (when struggling with what content to include in this book)

As opposed to *bad*? —we are programmed to think everything is either good or bad. Yet, most experiences are mixed.

Do I mean, 'I just want this to make me feel good'? Do I mean, 'be rich with factual content'? Do I mean 'be emotionally inspiring'? "Was it good?" or "Am I good?" are questions that ignore the richness of life. What "good" means is so subjective.

So, what *do* we mean when we say something is good or bad? Here, we must pause and reflect, maybe search for a better language to express what we mean. Once you start looking, you will find that binaries often cannot encompass what we really want to say.

That is why I am focusing on *dispelling* the binary.

Let's unpack this phrase a bit by looking at the definitions and etymology;

dis·pel
/dəˈspel/
verb

verb: **dispel**; 3rd person present: **dispels**; past tense: **dispelled**; past participle: **dispelled**; gerund or present participle: **dispelling**

1. To make (a doubt, feeling, or belief) disappear.

ie; "She found things to be grateful for in order to dispel her gloomy mood."
Origin

late Middle English: from Latin *dispellere*, from *dis-* 'apart' + *pellere* 'to drive'.
bi·na·ry

/ˈbīnərē,ˈbīˌnərē/
adjective
adjective: **binary**

1. relating to, composed of, or involving two things.

ie; " The ballot offered a binary choice without specifics."

1. something having two parts.
   ie; a binary star.

Origin

late Middle English (in the sense 'duality, a pair'): from late Latin *binarius*, from *bini* 'two together'.[1]

{ **2** }

On Dispelling

"If you want to find the secrets of the universe,
think in terms of energy, frequency, and vibration."

— Nikola Tesla, Engineer & Futurist

ABRACADABRA! — from the Aramaic, means "I create as I speak."

Our Words constantly create our experience of reality. They are spells. Language constructs and communicates meaning.

To spell is to create words that evoke images, feelings, and realities. Magic has always been about creating and altering reality.

Religion and science from all over time and space have spoken to everything in the universe being made of vibration, including you and me. All things are vibrating in different densities. We are affected by sound, tone, the words we hear and say, and the thoughts that repeat in our minds. To change our minds and state of being, we can begin by changing our thoughts, beliefs, and the words we use to describe our experiences of self and life.

Our common language often perpetuates the conditioning that makes us and our world sick with violence, chronic illness, and dependencies. Our words are spells. We are bombarded by media that intentionally create a trance of lack and need, which gives way to environments of judgment, competition, and xenophobia. Feelings of separation lead to fear and greed, grasping and hoarding. These conditions cause violence internally and in our shared environments. We do not need to live in fear. We each have the capacity to awaken to our fullness and interconnectedness, as demonstrated by the lives of many sages, saints, siddhis, yogins, and wisdom masters throughout time and space. The resources for wisdom and healing are more available to us than they have ever been.

Do your words in speech and thoughts harm yourself and others? To dispel something's power over us, we must pull back and see it for what it is, reframe it, or re-cognize it. I use this hyphenated spelling to heighten awareness of the inherent meaning of some words and how often we accept things simply because they are what we were taught growing up.

You have the power as an intelligent adult to see what spells of separation we have inherited. Take a step back and notice the views and experiences that binary thinking has promoted—question whether or not you believe these things and want to perpetuate them. You get to re-cognize, take the phrase, belief, or worldview, and investigate it from new perspectives. Is it true? How do I know this? Do I believe this? Would I *choose* this perspective? What other ways of looking at the situation are there? What beliefs or thoughts is *my* being vibrating with?

Are you under the spell of binary conditioning, feeling separate and judging yourself for what you perceive you are or are not?

I am not saying we need to *eliminate* all binaries! There will always be black and white, good and bad, men and women, zero and one, but binaries are so often used lazily, habitually, and divisively. At the same time, the colorful, varied in-between is neglected. This work invites you to awaken to where you have been held under spells of dichotomous thinking, divisiveness, other-ing, limiting beliefs, or archaic constructs of mind and dispel that shaizza!

Binaries are part of the non-dual, unified experience.

We do not attempt to delete the binary; we work to dispel its power over our minds, behaviors, relations, and worldviews. We practice watching our language and notice how our words affect our reality and others' responses to us.

We dispel and release the power of binary conditioning over our minds and lives.

Dispelling words, worldviews, behaviors, and beliefs that inhibit the full expression of life makes space for creativity and new life. Creativity is required to heal and build new lives.

We are not trying to jump to "all one," spiritual bypass-type thinking either. We are all different facets of the One, with differing views and experiences. Each of us holds a unique gift for each other.

The pain of separation that we all experience in one way or another must be recognized, felt, and dealt with individually and collectively as part of our healing.

We have the power to hold multiple realities at the same time, like feeling grief for a loss while at the same time feeling gratitude for the blessings of love that remain and flow newly into the space that loss has created. We could control our experience by steering ourselves towards joy every time we feel grief, but ultimately, this bypasses the necessary work of healing. True healing demands openness to all facets of our experience. Naming and *being with* the pain of loss (including injury and loss of feeling safe/seen/respected) is crucial to our healing. It is in all of our best interests to attend to old and new wounds to heal them and extract the medicine from the situation by our *presence* with the truth of the experience, ours and others, which may not always align but can be honored. Honoring is healing. The stories and words we use to represent our situation can make all the difference. Experiment with changing your language and create spells with your words for the more inclusive, compassionate, loving world you want to live in.

Binaries to Consider

Let's look at the specific binaries that have affected your experience. Check out the list below and notice which words resonate. Perhaps personal experiences or things you witness affecting those around you will arise. The simple act of acknowledging is a powerful tool for healing. Take some time with your journal to write your observations. If you are doing this work with a group, use these sets of binaries as a springboard for conversation. Add your own binaries

- *SELF / OTHER*
- *TOO MUCH / NOT ENOUGH*
- *BLACK / WHITE*
- *RICH / POOR*
- *WIN / LOSE*
- *GAY / STRAIGHT*
- *CLEAN / DIRTY*
- *WHOLE / BROKEN*
- *BEAUTIFUL / UGLY*
- *US / THEM*
- *PEACE / WAR*

- *GOOD / BAD*
- *SICK / HEALTHY*
- *RATIONAL / EMOTIONAL*
- *FACT / FICTION*
- *LIGHT / DARK*
- *CONSERVATIVE / PROGRESSIVE*

FACTS:

The binary of "good vs. bad" shapes how we view ourselves and others, but these rigid identifiers often lead to judgment and division within individuals and cultures. Studies by the National Institute of Mental Health on depression and cognitive distortions show that people with black-and-white thinking are more prone to negative mental health outcomes, including heightened depression and reduced emotional resilience. The National Alliance on Mental Illness (NAMI) estimates that over 16 million Americans experience depression annually, many exacerbated by internalized binary thinking about success or failure.

Journal Prompts

Journal prompts:

- How have you been affected by these ideas?
- What other binaries have you experienced or witnessed?
- Do binaries actually exist, or do we create them ourselves for the sake of doing less of the emotional and intellectual work we have to do when presented with choices?
- How might binaries limit your ability to grow and create?
- How can you dispel this conditioning?

"So much of this either/or mentality is at the root of the hard problems in politics, because first you divide..."
—*Vendana Shiva at the Consciousness Symposium, 2024*

{ 4 }

Deep Dive Into Some Binaries

Let's look a little deeper at some commonly suffered binaries. Below, I will highlight a few of the most insidious ones. Each could have its own book to break down how it shows up and its effects on us individually and culturally. None of these will be an exhaustive look. I hope you inquire further in your reflection, writing, and dialogue with others. Let my brief investigations be a starting point for your investigations. Remember that learning can come equally through resonance or friction.

If there are things that feel offensive to you, I encourage you to stay curious about them. We may have different experiences or worldviews, or perhaps a core wound or subconscious belief is being triggered. Look at "triggers" as gifts from your subconscious where you can. They usually point at something ready to be healed or changed.

{ 5 }

Good Or Bad?

Think of how many times you have been upset because something "bad" happened—you lost your job or your home, someone broke up with you, your car broke down, you missed your flight, etc. Yes, all of these things can really suck in the moment because it is not what we wanted or expected to happen, but then what happened? When we look back, we can often see that we learned something invaluable from that situation, or it pushed us forward out of a situation that was no longer serving our growth and thriving. Our animal bodies tend to panic when we lose those things they perceive as safety and security. With hindsight and the wisdom of experience we can see that, in our comfort, we would not have made the changes necessary for the arrival of unexpected opportunities and blessings. Perhaps you avoided an accident or met a key figure in your life due to those transportation challenges. With this reflection, take a moment to look back and reframe a situation.

Maybe next time you find yourself freaking out about an unwanted or unplanned happening such as these, you can stay curious and realize that it may not be that something "bad" is happening after all. Look for the good.

When a person shows up outside the expectations of authority, they are often punished for their differences, told that they are unacceptable in their natural expressions, that they are unworthy of love, and labeled as "bad" or "other." We see this happen in families, schools, workplaces, the judicial system—anywhere with a power-over type authority and an overarching culture that enforces conformity.

As children, or people-pleasing adults, we strive to show up how others want us to be in order to be loved and accepted. With this, we push our natural ways of being aside. The resulting divides, or cognitive dissonances, often lead to self-hatred, anxiety, and other mental health disturbances.

When we get the message that *we* are "bad" or that something is wrong with us the language of these reprimands and reproaches tends to cut and stick deeply in our psyche. It is important to be clear with yourself and others when *a behavior* is unacceptable as opposed to telling anyone that they are a *bad person*. The words that we hear become part of how we identify ourselves, for example, as a child, I was often reprimanded by my parents, "Shut up, big mouth! No one wants to hear that shit!" when expressing emotion or singing my little heart out. Over time, I shut up. I believed no one cared about how I felt or wanted to hear me sing. Obviously, (said my child mind) because how I felt didn't matter and I was bad at singing. This is what my child self, now 'inner child' learned from being talked to this way. So, I couldn't express my emotions or sing without shame and fear for a long time. Maybe my parents just needed quiet, but instead of telling me that, they said no one wanted to hear *me,* and that had a very different effect.

Have you ever been called a fuck up when you broke something or failed at something? Maybe your caretakers used a different phrase. Instead of addressing you with curiosity and empathy and using the mistake as a teaching experience, you were told that *you* were a failure. If we are taught that *we* are bad when we make mistakes, then that is what we learn rather than the lesson of the mistake. This is priming us to repeat the mistake.

This early learning can follow us through our lifetimes, so much so that when we do things later in life that we feel bad about, we end up feeling like a *bad person* instead of fairly reflecting on our *actions.* Herein, the shame spiral begins and perpetuates itself.

Shame and guilt are sticky emotions. They become attached to beliefs about ourselves, which then perpetuate themselves through stories and repeated behaviors as if we are trying to prove to ourselves and others that *we are* bad—that those authority figures who shamed us were right. The ego-mind will try to act out what it believes, whether or not those beliefs serve our well-being in the moment. Ego will try to "prove" whatever it believes by drawing situations and relationships to itself that confirm the belief. Yet, beliefs can be confronted and deconstructed. We can remember ourselves whole and worthy of love and success.

Mistakes aren't bad
They illuminate the path to success
Teach all the children
Inner & outer
that it is natural to make mistakes
This is how we learn
Learn to honor perceived failure
& grow adults with self-respect,
adults with the foundation for success.

Trying to be "good" is as much of a trap as thinking that we are "bad." Society imposes countless rules and expectations around what it means to be "good." Often, these derive from strict religious ideals. These expectations and ideals can set us up to fail. If we stopped pigeonholing people as either good/pure/above or bad/dirty/inferior, then we could all be more honest and dynamic. Our "good" people, such as parents, clergy, teachers, and leaders of all sorts, could just be human, acknowledge their feelings and impulses, and not act out on them in harmful ways because they repress the truth of their experience. We all have good and bad days, ways, and moments.

Were you taught to feel shame when you didn't fulfill your expected role(s) in life? When we begin to examine our social conditioning, we will likely first encounter shame. Learn to meet the confusion and shame that arises with curiosity and compassion. Often, when we are conditioned to feel ashamed, we project shame onto others, especially when they show up in ways that we don't think we can or should. When you witness another expressing life differently than you have been taught to, it might inspire judgment or shame. For example, having been raised to be a "good girl" and to "act like a lady", meaning to keep my mouth and legs closed, I noticed feelings of discomfort and judgment towards loud, openly sexual women. But honestly, I also had a strong attraction to these behaviors in others. Even if it is subconscious, we will want to reclaim the cut-off part of ourselves. We need to reclaim our cut-off parts in order to become whole. Wholeness is wellness. It is the goal of all healing processes. So, now I love brazenly expressive, sex-positive beings and am happy to be one myself.

> *"The weather is not good or bad, it just is. Rain might be inconvenient, disappointing, uncomfortable for some and welcome, needed or comforting for others."*
> - Paul Kivel, Author of "Living In the Shadow of the Cross"
> on the dualism of Christian moral binaries

SELF-INQUIRY

Take a moment to reflect on something you often judge others or yourself around.

Ask the following questions:

- Is it my shame that comes up, or is it someone else's?
- Is this my belief or someone else's belief that I inherited?
- Was I told that I was bad, wrong, or didn't belong, and now pass that judgment on to others?

Winner Or Loser?

R eframe the Failure

> *"Success is not final, failure is not fatal: it is*
> *the courage to continue that counts."*
> *--Winston Churchill*

Often, we try things and fail and never want to try them again because we hate to fail. We were likely taught that failure is bad. Even if we are blessed to have encouraging people around us, it can still be hard to overcome the feelings that arise when we are bad at something, especially if we are made fun of or chastised for it.

Here is an invitation to reframe your perceived failures. First, identify a story in which you felt like a failure and you want to reframe. Examine something that you felt or were told about yourself regarding this experience. It could be a self-limiting belief or a critical voice you heard from an authority figure that repeats in your head. Take some time to reflect on the experience you believed was a failure.

Reflect on what you learned or gained from this experience, even if it is as simple as — "This is how *not* to do something." Then, imagine you were going to lead a class based on the lessons you learned. Consider the following questions:

- Do you still believe what you "learned"?
- How is this belief affecting your life and those around you?
- Is this something you would *choose* to believe?
- Is it true?
- Is the opposite true?
- What else is true?
- Where can you give yourself credit, acknowledge, and appreciate the growth and learning in that experience?

Once you have taken some time to examine your "failure," it's time to reframe the story. Imagine that you are creating a class based on your experience. Brainstorm in your journal or use these questions as a jumping point for a conversation if you're doing this as a group. Use your creativity to expand the idea by answering the questions below.

- *What is the name of your class?*
- *How would students benefit from taking this class?*
- *What would students leave remembering about the class?*
- *What wisdom or advice could you share because of the experience you once considered a "failure"?*

Here is a small story as an example from my life that I have held close to my heart since reflecting on it as a grown-up.

I had a sewing teacher in my fashion design class in high school (I went to a vocational school); her name was Beatrice LaCroix. She wore grand, uniquely styled tent dresses she made for herself, all of the same silhouette with detailed patterns and couture embellishments. Her hands were gnarled with arthritis from years of tightly focused stitchwork. She was cranky in a French way and authoritative but kind. I didn't realize that last part at the time, as I was a crazy, rageful teenager who had a hard time seeing most authority figures as caring humans. For my senior collection, I was making a very fancy leather jacket. I worked hard to pay for the things I had; my family did not have money to pay for my fabrics.

I messed up on the sleeve of my coat and made a significant cut in the very center of it, with no more leather to spare. I freaked out. I was so distressed. I already held the story that I ruined everything. This situation just proved it. I was crying and very angry at myself. Mrs. LaCroix was so patient; I couldn't recall having experienced that kind of kindness when ruining something before. She told me, "The best art is made from mistakes." Then, she proceeded to help me get creative with ways to fix it. We ended up making the most fabulous sleeves, with an intricate pleated treatment and a stabilizing band that covered up the cut. Unless they took that thing apart, no one would know I had once ruined it. To this day, when something I am crafting goes sideways, I almost get excited right away, wondering what else it might become!

I learned so much that day about:

- Myself—I am not a failure; I am an artist and a healer. I can change the story.
- My dear teacher—She was not a fuddy-duddy old lady but a caring, creative soul.
- Creativity—is a process that often doesn't look like you think it will.
- How to stay curious in the creative process—Stay curious! Take a step back from the situation. Wonder, what else is possible? This advice applies directly to all of life.
- How to support others in their creative adventures—Acknowledge their distress, stay calm, offer inspiration, and let them find the solution.
- I cannot even count how many times I have supported others who were struggling with perceived failures in their creative processes by telling them what she told me, **"The best art is made from mistakes."**

That's the name of my class. It doesn't even need to be art that we are making, just mistakes. Then, we make art of them.

I have made art of my life due to living by this creed. Thank you, Mrs. LaCroix.

> *"Only those who dare to fail greatly can ever achieve greatly."*
> — *Robert F. Kennedy*

{ 7 }

Black Or White

Black-and-white thinking can refer to "all or nothing" thinking, also known as dichotomous thinking, and is discussed further in Chapter 9. It can also refer to manufactured divides based on skin color. These are not separate topics; they overlap. The "black or white" fallacy refers to a way of thinking wherein someone views a situation as having only two extreme options. This often shows up around race and ideological thinking and lends to more "with us or against us" type discourses, which continue to perpetuate binaries via shame and blame. This kind of thought and speech suppresses beneficial dialogue that could help to heal systemic inequities.

To lump people into "Black" or "White" categories is a prime example of how binary thinking ignores variation, complexity, and dynamism. While this may be obvious to many, one can easily forget, considering how these concepts have been reinforced in everyday media for many generations. Those referred to as Black can have ancestry originating anywhere in the vast continent of Africa. White usually refers to those of pale skin with genetic origins mainly in Europe.

Both groups include people who might have very different cultural experiences. Who is considered Black or White has also changed; from 1840 into the early 20th century, Celtic, Slavic, Iberian, *and* Hebrew people were considered Non-White. In reclaiming power from oppressive forces, reclaiming the language or slurs used against that group can be powerful. These terms can then name shared identities and communities. We witness that in generations of Black power movements, and I do not intend to disregard any of that here. But, we can never assume whether anyone identifies as Black or White or what that means about where they are from.

Race is a social construct. The construct of the white "race" was invented in 1676 by wealthy Virginians in the aftermath of what is known as "Bacon's rebellion," an uprising of poor, enslaved, and indentured Africans and Europeans. This invention of race was codified in the book *Systema Naturae* by Swedish naturalist Carl Linnaeus in 1735. Much ensuing pseudoscience continued to reinforce these false narratives that classified and divided people. The United States Supreme Court laws throughout the 1700s and 1800s went on to further institutionalize these claims and to subordinate people of color. Insidious laws gave wealthy, male, pale-skinned European colonizers justification for the stealing of land, genocide of indigenous humans, and the subjugation of other humans, especially dark-skinned people stolen from Africa, as enslaved people. White supremacists used false science and laws around race constructs to turn folx against each other and further the artifice of racial segregation well into the 1900s. In the so-called United States, governments did not overturn the last Jim Crow (enforced racial segregation) laws until 1965. Racially biased federal policies persisted until the 1970's. Remnants of these constructs and ways of thinking linger in many areas of the modern era. So much suffering has come from the deception of racial identifiers. The extremes of this thinking have caused people to be outrageously inhumane towards one another. We have come a long way, and there is a long way to go.

Fortunately, there is now a tremendous cultural wave of healing the ongoing impacts of slavery, anti-Black racism, and racialized capitalism. We are now reclaiming legacies of multi-racial coalitions to dismantle systemic oppression and center pro-Black lifeways and calls for reparations. Our work is ongoing. Our systems at large continue to keep us divided. It is up to each of us to acknowledge our complicity in the perpetuation of these systems and choose into the healing and transformation of oppressive systems. There are plenty of great books on the vital work of anti-racism and dismantling white supremacy, so I am not going to go too deeply into that here as my focus is on words and identity. I have listed some essential readings in the resource section at the back of this book.

It is crucial to acknowledge that a large and growing number of people in the West and around the world are of mixed heritage. Many of us carry the blood of both the oppressed and the oppressor. We will have different experiences in life based on our skin tone and other inherited factors. Yet, we are all of the human race. We are biologically the same. The

Human Genome Project in 2003 confirmed that humans are 99.9% identical at the DNA level and that there is no genetic basis for race.

Likely, many of you reading have had to check a 'Black' or 'White' box on some form at some time while feeling torn about whether you were negating some other part of yourself. How did that feel? How would you like to change that?

My Black cousins who grew up in rural New England were often asked ignorant questions about where they were from because their names were unfamiliar. They were from down the street. As far as I was concerned as a kid, they were all the same as me, including my step-siblings, who were Korean and dark-skinned Italian. We were all from the same family. I was often the odd one out, being so pale, sunburnt, and super allergic to poison ivy. I wished I was dark like them so that I wouldn't get made fun of for my skin's sensitivities. I had no idea of the privileges my pale skin would afford me, nor the challenges the rest of my family faced as a result of their skin tone. It took me years to notice that my cousins didn't have band-aids in their skin color or that we called the peachy-toned crayon "skin color" when that was not the skin color of half of my family!

I thought I wasn't racist or biased because I grew up in a multicultural family and saw us all as the same family sharing the same life. I have had to wake up to my ignorance. With ignorance comes participation in, and perpetuation of, white supremacy culture. It takes actively unlearning racist behaviors—catching these behaviors with relentlessness, humility, and self-compassion—to live into our anti-racist commitments. Just like yoga, it's both a somatic and a spiritual practice. May we all be aware of our involvement in systems we do not wish to adhere to or perpetuate. When awakening to this, I dove into books and courses on anti-racism and saw the structures and laws of the world anew. I believe that this is necessary work for white folx to do. As we collectively want to make change, we must see fully what we are working with.

A few years ago, hoping to connect with the lost roots of part of my lineage, I went to a Native American Health Center event near me. I visited the booths of local Indigenous craftspeople, and when I asked a merchant about a piece of shell jewelry, she said, "That's what we used as money before *you white people* came along." She rather spit that phrase, '*you white people.*' She lost that sale, and I walked away feeling ashamed and othered. I understand the pain, *and* I can never understand the pain. I feel grateful for being welcomed into tipi ceremonies in the area, but I have been reluctant to return to that community center. I am hesitant to even claim aloud my Indigenous heritage because of my pale skin. Yet, I know how my grandparents were affected by being, and denying, their Indigenous selves and how the pain and repression of that has trickled down through the generations. And, no matter what pains I have suffered due to the trauma and caste of my parents, our inherited traumas, or my sex, I live in a white supremacist culture and have not experienced undue suffering based on the color of my skin as most people of color in this culture have. This is important to remember.

What is a mixed-race person to do when living in a country where so many are taught to deny or erase their past? So many of us are cultural orphans with only "America" to pay our allegiance to. America needs some fixing. A lot of repair can come from evaluating and changing our habitual use of words, labels, constructs, and identities.

These experiences of mine are little things. Humbling things. I know I have benefitted in many ways from my pale skin and have not suffered as some of my ancestors or others in this world have. My pain could be dismissed as "white fragility;" nonetheless, we all must attend to our pain so that it doesn't eat us alive. We have all been damaged and divided by racism, classism, and caste. So many of us are cultural orphans without direct lines to our ancestors, languages, traditions, and homelands. We all have growth and healing to do. May we find connection rather than separation through our pain and healing.

In the future, I hope all humans will meet each other as equals in openness and honoring of one another. I wish for all people to have the right and place to express their hurt and ire—to be heard, seen, and honored for what they have lived through. There is a lot to be heard and healed. The wounds need to be attended to for the healing to happen. Healing can take time. We can't just jump into, "Yay, we are all happy and unified now!" as much as we might want that to happen. As with all grief and trauma, it is not a direct path to healing but a circuitous one requiring patience and persistence.

In the context of this work of dispelling the binary, we need to be open to the ongoing processes necessary to unwind from generations of violence and oppression.

Ultimately, there are vastly more places where we connect than not. The work required for us to move forward is again about curiosity, creativity, compassion, and welcoming the expansive nature of every being. Who we are goes far beyond our skin or genes.

"The tyranny of caste is that we are judged on the very things we cannot change, a chemical in the epidermis, the shape of one's facial features, the signposts on our body of gender and ancestry, superficial differences that have nothing to do with who we are inside. The caste system in America is 400 years old and will not be dismantled by a single law or any one person, no matter how powerful. We have seen in the years since the civil rights era that laws, like the voting rights act of 1965, can be weakened if there is not the collective will to maintain them. A caste system persists in part because we, each and every one of us, allow it to exist in large and small ways in our everyday actions, in how we elevate or demean, embrace, or exclude on the basis of the meaning attached to people's physical traits. If enough people buy into the lie of natural hierarchy, then it becomes the truth or is assumed to be. Once awakened, we have a choice."

— Isabel Wilkerson, *Caste, The Origins of Our Discontent.*

(I believe this book is vital for understanding the roots of racism in America and I encourage you to read it.)

REFLECTION PROMPTS

- How have you benefitted or struggled due to the color of your skin?
- Have you ever felt confused about whether you were black or white or what heritage to claim or hide?
- Have you or your family hidden who they were or stopped speaking their inherited language in attempts to assimilate into a homogenized culture?
- What experiences have you had around the construct of race or caste that have affected who you are? In what ways would you like things to be different?

Man vs Nature

"There is more to us than we know. If we can be made to see it, perhaps for the rest of our lives we will be un-willing to settle for less."

—Kurt Hahn, educator & creator of Outward Bound

Nature can be fierce. It is easy to feel separate from nature when we have to protect ourselves from it. We've all had to "battle the elements" to some extent, our ancestors even more so. Self-preservation has set us up in opposition to nat-ural forces; thereby, a long-standing binary persists as Man vs. Nature. Binary thinking in this context developed as a primal survival response. Historically, for primitive humans in the natural world, choices in the moment could mean life or death. Thus began the path of man moving toward dominating na-ture rather than learning to live in harmony with it.

City living and technology-focused lives have caused a fur-ther disconnection from nature and, therefore, critical aspects of ourselves. This divorce includes the loss of connection to healing powers and medicines provided directly from natural sources. By not knowing or being in harmony with nature, we have set ourselves up for disconnection from our well-being and the health of our environments. Self-destructive systems have been created, which show up as everything from our systems of "healthcare" being geared more towards sick care, to toxic food growth and production, oppressive legal and financial systems, lack of access to communal resources, climate change, and the environmental devastation that is happening via extreme weather events. Our systems, built on the false divide between humans and nature, are failing us.

The neglect and destruction of natural ecosystems by governments, big business, and the exceedingly wealthy lowers the quality of life for all of us. This separatist, othering behavior causes toxicity in our earthly, social, and economic ecosystems. Our primal fears are now being poked at as we experience the devastating effects of climate change, war, and extremism. Binary thinking is perpetuated and elevated in these states of fear, as we are witnessing in the current sociopolitical environments worldwide.

Lumping things or people into boxes or extreme ends of a spectrum is not easy on us or our planet. This kind of separatist thinking leads to the collapse of cultures, ecosystems, and personal relationships. If we approach any relationship with an all-or-nothing, binary mindset, there is a fifty percent chance we end up with nothing.

We have evolved in many ways; in others, we have remained frightened, stuck animals. Yet, we have the means to make life-saving connections. In this age of advanced transportation, communication, mass production, factory farming, abundance, and knowledge, it should be clear that there is enough for everyone. Scarcity could be a thing of the past, yet we continue to have scarcity thinking.

We need to deconstruct the constructs of mind that inhibit the sharing of resources. Nature shows us how. If we use the systems we have to *connect* all beings to what they need, it would be possible to feed and house the world. Instead of wealth for the few and the oppression of the majority, we could have well-being for all. We must consider our interconnectedness on all fronts, remember ourselves as part of nature, and one another as extensions of ourselves, in order to survive. We got a magnified glimpse of our interconnectedness during the COVID-19 pandemic when everything stopped for a while in lockdown. Air and waterway pollution began to clear. Wild animals came out into the vacated, once-bustling streets to explore spaces that were usually too dangerous for them. A study on pollution by Boston University's School of Public Health revealed that ultrafine particle concentration in the air dropped by nearly 50% due to reduced aviation and road activity in the first few months of the pandemic.[2]

Living in this world now can feel overwhelming, with so many pressing environmental and social issues. Likely, you want to do *something*, but choosing what is most important and *how to make a difference* can feel impossible. The same work needs our attention on all levels, micro to macro.

When we feel disconnected from nature, we can be blind to our effects on it—so we litter, overproduce, overconsume, have unsustainable waste systems, and suffer the consequences.

As many wise beings have said, when anyone suffers, we all suffer. Rigid identifiers can keep us feeling separate and enable violence toward the perceived other, including nature. Mindful attention to our connectedness is the medicine for that and for so many of our ails.

She is speaking loudly now. Mother Nature is calling us home to clean up our messes, or, so it seems, she will do it for us.

Beneath us is a fantastic web of physical life holding us all together. The roots of the trees and mycelium (a network of tubular filaments which are the vegetative structure of fungus) intermingle to create a worldwide web (or wood-wide web, as the witches say) of communication and connection to resources.

In a 2020 video on mycelium[3], National Geographic said that this network connects at least 90% of the trees and plants on earth. This mycelial system breaks down organic matter and helps to facilitate nutrient exchange between plants. There is an incredible wealth of science, supposition, and poetry about mycelium, which I won't go into here, but I encourage you to seek it out. Here, I point to this wonder of nature as it informs and instructs our natural reality. We are all interconnected in this same way with one another, with earth, spirit, and all parts of ourselves. We need one another. We are an ecosystem. To have healthy environments we must tend with care to all of the constituents of our shared garden home, Earth. We thrive best in environments that remember and support this. Yet, so much of our current environment ignores or even negates this. Together, we have the power to change this current paradigm.

Earth-based spiritualities and yoga/Tantra teach that understanding how nature works is to understand ourselves better. Our relationship with what we call nature is a micro/macrocosmic situation. We are nature. Witness how your environment, the weather, seasons, and the cycles of the celestial bodies influence you. Understand that we, too, are part of and affected by these cycles.

The work highlighted in this book is the work we can do in our inner microcosms to free ourselves individually. The same work needs to be done by our world communities on the global level. We must find unity in our diversity and honoring of the perceived "other" if we hope to find resourceful ways to support surviving and thriving on this planet for all beings. The healing invitation is to recognize the Self that *you are* and that *is you* in all beings: people, animals, plants, and elements.

We are not separate. We are inextricably interconnected. Immersing in the natural world can teach, heal, and remind us of who we are and how to live in a good way that honors and supports thriving.

> "*In some Native languages the term for plants translates to "those who take care of us.*"
> —*Robin Wall Kimmerer, Braiding Sweetgrass*

"Man is a part of nature, and his war against nature is inevitably a war against himself."
—*Rachel Carson, environmentalist*

{ 9 }

Create To Honor Creation

Take some time to commune with nature. Realize your place in it. I have suggested some activities below. Let these become part of your practice and part of your life. Actively become part of nature and let nature express itself through you.

- **Create a nature altar.** Go on a walk in nature and collect bits or photos of things that inspire and/or that you might usually overlook. Tune into the worlds within worlds that are happening all around us. Combine these in a collage or altar that reminds you of your inherent connectedness.
- **Observe the cycles of nature.** Observe the lifecycle of a plant or season and overlay an experience, a stage of life, or a relationship in your personal life over this cycle. See how this can help to make sense of things. All of life has cycles and seasons. Find bits that represent death, decay, giving back, transformation, new life, beauty, hope, or anything that inspires you to slow

down and see your experience of life reflected in the life around you.

- **Explore Creative Expression.** Make some visual art or write a poem relating the natural world's cycles to your personal experiences. Notice how nature is teaching us about life all the time.
- **Get your hands in the dirt.** Start a garden, plant a plant, study herbalism or our food and waste systems.

{ 10 }

Binary Thinking & Trauma

FACT: Gender and race divides were constructed in order to oppress and control.

> "...these binaries are false binaries that oppress all people, men and women alike. Cis people by depriving them of a full range of experience and expression. Trans people by violence. Women by sexism and violence. The poor through invisibility. People of color through racial oppression."
>
> —Jane Arc; yoga student, trans woman, engineer, seminarian

A traumatic experience can be defined as one in which the nervous system gets overwhelmed and doesn't know how or isn't able to protect itself from danger. When our nervous systems are overwhelmed we lose our ability to *choose a response.* Instead, we tend to react from our animal nature in order to protect ourselves from what is perceived as life-threatening. This can show up as variations on fighting, freezing (playing dead), fawning (becoming submissive), or fleeing (running away/hiding). These are known as trauma responses.

Sometimes, the trauma is ongoing, as with a generally hostile home, school, or social environment that feels threatening and dangerous. This is often referred to as a little "t" trauma, where there is not one big incident but ongoing hostilities that cause similar responses in the nervous system. Then there are the big "T" traumas, often singular incidents of direct danger/ violence that feel life-threatening in the moment and cause one to freeze, fight, flee, or fawn. When this happens, our nervous system kicks into survival mode and is purely focused on staying alive until it feels safe again.

Sometimes, we can return to an evidently safe environment but not *feel* safe for a long time. This is a trauma response, and anything that relates to the original occurrence can trigger it. When this response is ongoing, it is referred to as post-traumatic stress disorder or PTSD. With PTSD, the nervous system "alarm" stays on and is hyper-aware, looking for danger everywhere so that what happened before does not happen again. The emotions and impulses that resulted from the initial situation will wait to be dealt with at another time once the perceived threat has been handled. In the moment of the original occurrence the system is overcome with trying to protect or save the life of the body. Likely, it will feel scary to deal with the feelings that arise later, as dealing with them often triggers the panic of the original occurrence. So, the organism/ nervous system creates protections to help us avoid experiencing the trauma again. These protections can look like anger issues, timidity, denial, numbing out, dissociation, dependencies, suicidal thoughts, risky behaviors, etc...

The subconscious mind wants to complete the desired pattern of protection that it was unable to complete at the time of the trauma (i.e., standing up for ourselves or escaping danger). This might lead to seeking out or creating situations or relationships that have similarities to the initial occurrence of trauma. For example, we might find ourselves attracted to and dating people who have many of the same qualities, behaviors, or wounds as our parents with whom we have unresolved issues. This tendency for the subconscious to recreate similar situations in order to complete an incomplete protective pattern can show up as personality traits, habits, defenses, dissociation, anxiety, depression, and aggression. Often one will begin to identify with these patterns, as in believing, "This is just how I am". We heal from these self-defeating patterns when we feel the feelings from the original occurrence that needed to be felt and practice owning our power, voice, and bodily autonomy in safe and supported settings.

As we examine our ideas of who we are or who we feel we are "supposed to be," it is important to reflect on how our environment and experiences have molded our identities. Noticing and re-cognizing (rethinking, re-perspecting) are key practices to healing and dispelling limiting beliefs.

Healing is a process of re-membering, bringing all the parts of ourselves back together. We call back our exiled parts, the parts of ourselves and our communities that have been estranged due to judgments and expectations that caused them not to fit into the accepted narratives. The pain of separation and division teaches us and calls us to reunite.

It takes courage and hard work for us to come into our full selves, especially in the wake of traumas inflicted upon us *and* our ancestors, which may still be affecting us years and generations later. The memories of trauma and the protective behaviors borne of it can be inherited through our DNA and pre-verbal learning. It takes courage, vigilance, and perseverance to heal these patterns. We must find places to express ourselves and connect to others in new, safer environments. Every time we take a risk and are held and honored in a caring way, we move toward growth and healing. Connection is the medicine.

Rejecting the status quo, healing trauma, and reclaiming the freedom of trusting one's own intuition, self-knowing, and authentic self-expression takes courage, vigilance, and dedication.

To heal from imposed traumas such as being rejected for who we are (often via racism, sexism, homophobia, transphobia, or institutional violence enacted against us or our family due to our cultural identifiers), we must acknowledge the constructs of mind and culture that have enabled or enforced these constructs. The harm done needs to be recognized. Then, we can give all the support possible to those disenfranchised and dismantle these constructs. It is time to embrace our diversity as a human family focused on the wellness of our people and planet.

When we address our personal and inherited traumas, we begin to heal and transmute them. We bring the disparate parts of ourselves back together and become integrated beings who are able to take responsibility for how we show up. How we show up affects our own lives and others.

> *"What is troubling about our conceptions of binaries is the value judgment that always accompanies them. Because one pole must be judged as superior to the other, inferiority is a necessary result, and disparate ideas and symbols come to be understood as oppositional rather than complementary.*
>
> *... It is through careful examination of our epistemologies and their relationship to our identities and our conceptualizations of others that we can begin to shift them to become more inclusive, more humanizing, and more fluid. This is work that must be done both in individual minds and hearts and together as a collective."*
>
> —"FROM GOOD VS. EVIL TO RATIONAL VS. EMOTIONAL: A DISCUSSION OF BINARIES OF KNOWLEDGE AND THOUGHT" by Rebecca Shamash, University of Minnesota

FACTS:

Binary thinking amplifies trauma, especially for those in marginalized communities. For example, transgender and non-binary individuals are nearly four times more likely to experience PTSD compared to the general population, according to the UCLA Williams Institute's Transgender Mental Health Disparities Report. Systemic oppression rooted in binaries—such as "man vs. woman" or "Black vs. White"—creates environments of chronic stress that further harm mental health. Data from the American Journal of Public Health (2018) shows that 60% of adults in marginalized groups report symptoms of trauma tied to identity-based discrimination.

Reflection: Re-Cognizing Binary Conditioning

The intention of this work is to expand our awareness and language to be more inclusive and connective rather than alienating and harmful. We have the power to heal these manufactured divides. When we learn to celebrate our own dynamism, it becomes natural to see and appreciate the dynamic richness of others. Humanity is a brilliant jewel with facets that sparkle and shine. Each facet has a different shine and perspective, yet is an integral part of the whole. It is the dynamism of life that makes it dazzling!

To re-cognize something is about looking at things from new perspectives. It is practice; it is play. As you complete these exercises, I encourage you to be compassionate with yourself, remain curious, and approach the process with as much playfulness as possible. This is courageous, creative work.

Reflect and Share - for journaling and dialogue

Ask *yourself* these questions first, and do some writing and reflection. Then, engage in these inquiries with others to explore how breaking free from binary thinking might help you and others grow and connect. When you open conversations with friends and community about how binary thinking affects *your* life, the dialogue will naturally expand beyond personal reflections, and you will find new places of connection and inspiration.

- *Have you been hurt or inhibited due to binary conditioning?*
- *How have you hurt others due to binary judgments?*
- *Have you been kept from expressing the fullness of your true self?*
- *Have you inhibited others from expressing themselves authentically?*

Are there times when your thoughts, words, or questions are framed in an absolutist or binary way? Could this be hurting you or others? Some examples include:

- "I am a good person/a bad person"
- "I am sick/well"
- "They are right/wrong"
- "I never/always"

"to overcome binary thinking, we need a *willful/conscious effort to decide/create a middle path* rather than accept a given set of binary choices."

From *The Theory of the Third—How to Overcome Binary Reasoning, and "Good vs Evil" by Ed Alvarado*[4]

{ 12 }

Spectrums of Possibility

"Practically everything we see and measure in space, not only objects but temperature, size, density is on a spectrum...In fact, the very word spectrum comes from what happens when you take light and break it up into its colors. We just happen to assign names to the seven colors - red, orange, yellow, green, blue, indigo, violet, but it's a continuum... We're just being lazy by assigning seven colors. Our brain doesn't want to see nuance because it's easier for us to think in binary. Are you with me or are you against me? Well, maybe you're somewhere in between. Are you a boy, are you a girl? Maybe they're expressing themselves somewhere in between, and your brain has a difficult time recognizing a spectrum, and so you're requiring it be into a bin, so there you are forcing other people to match how you see the world...

The world is not gonna change to fit your inability to recognize how it's actually manifesting."

\- astrophysicist, Dr. Neil deGrasse Tyson

Our cultural conditioning is permeated by binary thinking on every level.

No blanket true/false binary exists for anyone. What we experience is a nuanced, variable, shifting perspective based on the environment and time. We are all multi-dimensional beings living multi-dimensional lives. Giving ourselves and one another space to be honest and aware of these fluctuations is a great gift.

There are spectrums on which we all exist that have apparent opposites or constellations of gathered, relative qualities, but these can quickly turn from one into the other. Different qualities of being will dominate depending on our environment, the people we are with, the place we are in, whether our basic needs have been tended to, the time of life, year, or day. Boxing anything in with an either/or label does not serve aliveness.

When I say that I am devastated by grief
But overflowing with blissful love for life
Or
When I say I am conservative with whom I intimately share myself
But that I also believe in free love
Am I lying?
Do we not often hold more than one truth or perspective on things?

"Do I contradict myself? Very well then I contradict myself,
I am large, I contain multitudes."
- Walt Whitman, poet

Have you noticed what happens when people are not honest about their natural human complexities? When people strive to be a certain way to gain approval, they deny or exile other parts of themselves, repressing related thoughts or impulses. Eventually, those aspects become perverted (meaning corrupted or distorted from their original course, meaning, or state) and eventually they surface in inadvertent, surreptitious ways that can be toxic to ourselves and those around us.

Enantiodromia - en-an-ti-o-dro-mia - /əˌnan(t)ēə'-drōmēə/ noun,
The tendency of things to change into their opposites, especially as a supposed governing principle of natural cycles and psychological development.
—from Oxford Language Dictionary

The Swiss psychoanalyst Carl Jung applied the concept of enantiodromia to such psychological phenomena, meaning that when one-sided tendencies dominate conscious life, an equally powerful counterposition builds up[5]. Nietzsche and Heraclitus are also quoted, making references to how too much of one force can create an opposing reaction.[6]

Examples of Enantiodromia:

- We ignore our individual or communal health until we come to a crisis point that requires us to prioritize that health
- We continually give to or sacrifice for others until we hit a breaking point of resentment and reactivity
- Sexually conservative or abstinent spiritual leaders behaving as sexual predators
- "Nice" girls acting out in cruelty or promiscuity
- Anti-gay crusaders found to be in secret, intimate gay relationships

If people had a place to talk about their urges or thoughts without being demonized, then they would be less likely to act on repressed desires, and any harmful impulses could be dissolved in the light of awareness rather than grow further distorted in secrecy and shame. When I gave my long-term rockstar partner permission to have his dream experience, including being intimate with other people on tour, it turned out he did not want to act that way. It might have been an enticing opportunity if it had been restricted. Yet, with permission, he had the space to reflect and realized there was no appeal. This recognition reminded us that humans tend to want what they can't have. Not acknowledging and honoring desires, painful experiences, or things we are not "supposed to" feel creates shame, which tends to cause hiding and/or acting out. Repression breeds perversion. As it is said, 'what we resist persists' in one way or another. To highlight this further, there is also, as aforementioned, the psychological concept of enantiodromia, where when we go so far into one pole on something it inevitably gives way to its opposite. This happens within our societal constructs as well as our individual experiences, which are often inextricable influences. The antidote for this? Dispel binary thinking.

When we dissolve the rigid concepts of either/or, good/bad, and instead, say, "yes, and..." we can have the courage to admit the whole picture of Self. Our ideal selves can unify with the reality of our nuanced minds, and our animal nature can dance with our spiritual nature. We can live fully, love fully, and heal in the light of truth.

As I have learned to embrace the fullness of my being and the many facets of "me", I have found so much peace in life. Instead of being defeated by reflexive habits of defensiveness, blame, numbing out, rebellion, willfulness, hopelessness, etc. I am able to see the cycles and rhythms of being that are naturally flowing and *choose* to dance with them. This acceptance and courage to *be* with what is has brought deep healing and integration. In the course of this—acting, fashion, circus, drag, and moving through different states and social circles have all been avenues of self-discovery. To create and find places and ways to *play* with the feelings and possibilities of 'self' has become of foremost importance to me in this life for myself and as a gift to others. Giving myself permission to create characters, to dance with my many 'selves', and to be honest and unashamed about the experiences that I have had in this body and mind has been truly life-saving and life-giving.

Along this path of discovery there have been practices and games which I thought I made up. They were playful combinations of acting, yoga, and therapy, which I found through experience, go hand in hand. Years after inviting others to join me in playful yoga/theatre games led by an alter-ego character of mine, I learned from those witnessing and participating that this mode of play already existed. It is a practice of Tantrik yoga to ritualize the play of embodying one's fears and trickster/daemon aspects in order to dispel their power. See the ritual exorcise (word play to highlight how playing with something can dispel its power), "Angels & Demons" in the spells and rituals section at the back of the book for an instructed invitation to play with your various selves. It is natural for us to have and curiously engage with aspects of ourselves in our inner world as well as see others as aspects of our self in the outer world.

Internal Family Systems[7] is a modern, systematic way of communing with the many aspects of self as well. It is a non-pathologizing, evidence-based psychotherapy that, like yoga philosophy, acknowledges an internal, unbreakable "Self" and helps the client get to know this Self. It also works with each being as a system of protective and wounded "parts", affirming that the mind is a thing of multiplicity. It is of great relief to those of us who have known or wondered why we have "so many voices in our heads" that it is perfectly "normal" after all to do so. What is not "normal" is suppressing those parts and impulses so much that they eat us alive from the inside or cause us to act out on the most harmful of them. I put "normal" in quotes because it is also a harmful binary to think that we are either "normal" or not normal/that something is wrong with us. I use this word because it is a common vernacular, and most of us are conditioned to worry about whether we are normal or not. It is normal to have self-doubting thoughts, and not necessary to believe them.

IFS (Internal Family Systems) refers to parts of ourselves that were developed to help us survive and thrive in challenging or hostile environments. The parts are divided into two primary categories: protectors and exiles, and the protectors are further divided into managers and firefighters. The parts want to be there for you, the Self, but sometimes they don't know how to help us as they were most often developed as children, and thus try to help in maladaptive ways. Sometimes, these parts last far beyond their expiration dates—meaning they are still trying to run the show even after we no longer need them. For example, "protector parts" might be trying to control emotions, identity, or self-expression for the (perceived) safety of the Self. Once we see that this (part) is not "me," but a way of being that may have been necessary for a time, then we can dialogue with the part and let them know, "I am ok and do not need to think or act in these ways anymore." We can dialogue with the inner and outer voices that would otherwise try to silence us, informing them that we are so much more than one perspective or experience can reveal. For example, instead of believing the inner voices that criticize and admonish, I now say to my brain, "Thank you, brain. But now I am choosing to see things another way." And I repeatedly replace those thoughts with their opposite or my current intention. With practice, we can then go forth with courage and curiosity, not rejecting or denying any of our experience. We can integrate all of it, heal, and grow into our inherent fullness and ease. To me, IFS is a modern proof and remedy for the harm caused by rigid identifications and denial of the multifaceted self that is an outgrowth of binary thinking.

"It's the normals that made normality the norm"
Dr. Hal of the Church of the Subgenius quoting Rev. Stang in the movie "*Arise*"

{ 13 }

Self-Concepts

"I am less and less a creature of influences in myself which operate beyond my ken in the realms of the unconscious. I am increasingly an architect of self. I am free to will and choose. I can, through accepting my individuality, my 'isness,' become more of my uniqueness, more of my potentiality."

— Carl R. Rogers, *Person to Person: The Problem of Being Human*

Your self-concept is who you believe you are. This includes;

- The public self: the view defined by others' knowledge of you
- The actual or behavioral self: created by your actions and habits
- The aspirational self: who you aspire to be
- Your self-image: how you see yourself physically and cognitively
- Your self-esteem: formed by the interactions and feedback that you got from others throughout your life, especially in your formative years.

The layers of your being are physical, mental/emotional (also called "energetic" in the yogic view), social, and spiritual. Self-concept is generally a wide view of who you are on all these levels of being. We interact with and relate to these layers in ever-changing ways over time. The ideas we have about who we are on each of these layers are formed and adjusted as we grow, based on our experiences and the information we gather about ourselves from the reflections and input by the people around us. Note that what we "learn" is not always "truth".

As beings of spirit born into bodies, we all have some inner dividedness. In learning about our bodies, we learn to differentiate Self from others and the environment. On one hand, there is how we perceive, relate to, and innately see ourselves. Then, there is how we come to identify ourselves in relation to others. With that, there is how we learn we are "supposed to be", by way of societal and familial conditioning. In Rogerian therapy, these selves are called the "real self" and the "ideal self"—how one naturally is and how they are told they should be. When these two are far apart from each other, the incongruence caused by this split can run deep. It can lead to dysphoria, depression, and anxiety, all of which can result in dependencies and other psycho-emotional disorders, including psychotic breaks and schizophrenia.

Rogerian & humanistic psychology is largely based on the concept of the "ideal" and "real self". These refer to how we are taught to be as opposed to how we naturally are. Our 'real' self is us as children, living in wonder, playfulness, curiosity, and uninhibited, unpretentious self-expression. The 'ideal' self is what we are taught we're "supposed to be".

Carl Rogers was one of the founders of Humanistic Psychology. He broke away from conventional, authoritative models of therapy with his own compassionate style, borne of observations in his practice beginning in the 1940's. Humanistic Psychology informs many modern approaches to therapy. Rogerian therapy became referred to as client or person-centered therapy. The basis of its philosophy is to center and meet the individual client where they are, with unconditional positive regard, rather than from the position of a dominating authority figure. Psychotherapy today has integrated much of Rogers' approach.

For Rogers, each being is their own authority, knowing how to best heal themselves. The job of the therapist is to guide them back to their own knowing through non-judgemental listening and reflecting. Each knows best what made them who they are and knows best how to become the person they want to be. We don't heal ourselves alone, of course. One's seeing can become occluded and clarity can be supported by way of others' attentive listening and reflection. Each person's healing journey may look different and can be supported by many external influences: doctors, therapists, coaches/counselors, communities, and nature itself. These all help as guides along the path, just as supports are used to help new plants grow. We are each other's fertilizer, support structures, shade, sun, and rain...

We need each other. Our need for each other is further proof that we are all more than our limited-in-perception, individual selves. We are all, all of it. We are an interconnected web of being. Through every choice we make, we influence one another's well-being. Our choices of words, thoughts, and behaviors all affect each other. What we take in, what we believe, and what we focus on, repeat, or ignore has an effect on our own psyche and on how others experience us. This all ultimately reflects back and influences how we see ourselves.

When we learn from our environment that we are not as we are "supposed to be" or as expected to be, this can affect our self-concept. The inner critic, that voice we all have in our heads, policing us—telling us that we are doing it wrong, should be working harder, are stupid, unworthy, not fitting in, or other things like that—stems from our earliest impressions, the messages that we received from our parents, authority figures, and social conditioning. This voice has the job of trying to keep us safe, helping us to watch out for the worst possible outcomes. Yet, the source of this voice was often misguided and uninformed. We might stop to realize that this inner critic doesn't serve our thriving at all. Often we will even hear ourselves repeating the things that others said to us that we hated hearing. Sadly, sometimes, this voice creates the worst outcomes by debilitating us with fear, insecurity, and self-hatred.

This is where the reminder that **we do not have to believe our thoughts** can be helpful. Neither what we are told nor what we think necessarily equals truth. As we get to know ourselves and observe our thoughts and behaviors, we can choose to change them. Therefore, we can change how we feel, see ourselves, and our self-concept.

In my personal experience and in healing practice with others, I have found that *identification* is a primary cause of suffering. As in, "I am this, not that, I don't.., I can't..," etc. We have been held under the spell of what we are "supposed to be'" on so many levels that we do not even know what our own experience of self *can* look like.

When we are told that we are or are not something, especially over and over again, we come to believe it. Often, this information comes from our own head in the form of internal dialogue or intrusive thoughts. This thought usually has roots in something someone told us in the past, especially if the memory is traumatic. Stories that we "learned" during traumatic periods leave the deepest scars. In Sanskrit, the language of yoga, this scar is called a 'samskara', also meaning a "groove" or "path". Samskaras are not only formed in traumatic situations. They are formed from the impressions left by our actions, including what we spend our time thinking about, which can affect our whole experience of life. Samskaras tend to become our go-to habits physically and emotionally. Yogic psychology describes this as returning repeatedly to the feelings and beliefs that were seeded during formative and traumatic moments. As in, "I suck at this" (belief/story), or, "Every time I try to...I fuck it up". With this belief and the associated feelings that arise whenever a similar situation comes up, we find ourselves, in fact, failing at what we are afraid of failing at again and again until we find a way to shift our perspective, belief, and the stories/words being repeated in our head.

The yogic teaching of samskara refers to a neural pathway, a thought or behavior pattern that has been developed over time or via a traumatic experience. The more that we tread any pathway, the deeper it becomes, just like a path through a field or woods. The more often that we repeat or act out any belief or thought pattern, the more likely we are to fall onto that path again, even to the point where it becomes a default. This phenomenon contributes to the building of an identity, as repetition of the pattern deepens an individual's association with the pattern until it becomes ingrained as the individual's idea of "this is just who I am" or "how I am". It is the way of the human mind to grasp onto story, meaning, identity, and belonging, including "identifying" as a failure or "belonging" as an outcast. Any identifier born of any experience can become a point of reference for the perceived separate self. Our minds try to pin down what is beyond our senses' grasp or that which we can only *point* towards, like our sense of "self", with words. We are story-making machines. Knowing this, we can grow our awareness and apply our wisdom to what words we use, what stories we tell, and, therefore, what realities we are perpetuating.

As individuals, if we ignore or shamefully hide any part of ourselves, it will come out later as resentment, rage, or sickness. If we as families, communities, or cultures cast judgment or shame onto someone or a group of others, then they, too, will eventually become a volatile force to be reckoned with. As an extreme example, we see this showing up throughout time as war, taking place between violently oppressed people who rise up against the oppressor and the more powerful oppressor nation committing atrocities in an attempt to wipe out the people perceived to be a threat or in their way.

No part of any living entity can be ignored without it eventually causing illness. Other-ing is a wound that creates pain that increases over time until it cannot be ignored. Our planet is crying out this lament as well. We are being called to awaken to our interconnectedness on all levels of being.

Everyone wants to belong. Everyone does belong.

Individuals create community, and community creates culture. We are a community of spirit with the potential to change the overarching culture. It is up to all of us to create the new narrative together. This begins with staying curious, embracing, and learning about ourselves and one another as aspects or mirrors of our Self.

"If you bring forth what is within you, what you bring forth will save you. If you do not bring forth what is within you, what you do not bring forth will destroy you."
—Jesus, From the Gospel of Thomas, 70

Journal Prompts

- Are limiting beliefs or poisonous thoughts inhibiting your freedom, self-love, and acceptance?
- What beliefs do you have about yourself based on others' rules about life or their responses to you over your lifetime?
- What is on repeat in your psyche?
- Did you choose these thoughts? Do you want to change them?
- How can you now choose to re-parent or re-pattern yourself with new thoughts, habits, and behaviors?
- What could you accept about yourself that you have historically resisted?

{ 14 }

Meditation for
Self-Acceptance

R ead through the following meditation and fill in the
blanks to personalize it. Record yourself reading it, or
listen to my recorded version which you can access via the QR
code in the "Use This Book" section in the back of the book.

*Sit back in a comfy seat and listen. If writing or drawing helps
you, that's okay, too. Take a few deep breaths to center and land into
this intentional meeting with your Self and your parts.*

*Conjure up an image or physical feeling of being held and nur-
tured. Perhaps you wrap your arms gently around yourself. Maybe
you can invoke a feeling of someone who you feel or have felt really
safe with and nourished by. Tune into the energy of feeling held, nourished, loved, seen, and supported...*

Breathe into this energy or imagining...

*After a bit, let the images of anyone outside of yourself melt away
and just become present with the energy of feeling held in a caring,
healing way.*

Welcome your inner child, or some part of your being, into your gentle embrace. Breathe together in that embrace. Continue to invoke the nurturing, caretaker energy, and direct this energy to the part of yourself that you are communing with. If this is hard, perhaps you could think of a soothing aspect of nature, divinity, or any other creature you have witnessed or felt as a loving, accepting presence. Allow the feelings of love and acceptance to expand and become your primary focus. Breathe into it, and let that energy of care commune with any part of you that could use this energy.

Notice that you have easy, spacious breaths or invite them to become so. Become aware of your steady heartbeat.

Hold yourself gently and lovingly. Notice whatever thoughts or emotions are present. Continue to non-judgmentally hold and love your self and whatever arises.

Press pause and simply practice sitting and holding yourself with unconditional loving acceptance for as long as it feels right.

That could be enough for now...

Or, Go Deeper—

Bring to mind a moment of hearing or experiencing something with an authority figure or parent that you wished you hadn't. Connect to the way that this memory or story lives in your body. Notice how we perpetuate feelings by repeating certain words, thoughts, images, or stories to ourselves - often, these show up as our inner critic. Become present with the emotions that these thoughts or stories stir up.

Sit and hold that inner critic, or the present feelings connected with a past experience, with unconditional loving awareness.

Sense that this voice/thought/feeling was formed a long time ago and not by your choice. It may or may not be very clear exactly where this voice or any particular thoughts or phrases came from. It doesn't really matter in the end, as long as you are willing to hold the resulting part of you kindly.

Send love to whatever is present. Soften into being present with it, make space around it with your breath, and love it for what it is.

Thank this part for working to protect you. Acknowledge as much as you can that this is what it has been trying to do in its own way. Ask that voice instead to receive the gift of knowing [... an inspiring opposite of the current feeling...]. Tell your young self with love and even playfulness that you no longer have to think that way and that what you are now choosing to focus on is [...fill in w/ yours...]

Doing this regularly, even simply gently holding yourself, will help you develop and recognize yourself as your own refuge and deepen the space of loving care within you.

It can be challenging to meet these voices, so do this slowly and with easier things first before moving on to more intense experiences. Whatever voices arise, remember that they have been put in place in an effort to protect you. By becoming repeated thoughts, they have become beliefs. These beliefs are in place with the (misguided) intention to keep you safe, so there will likely be parts of you that will resist changing them. There may be fierce resistance, even so much so that they try to reinforce themselves with inner narratives or outer behaviors. Stay non-judgmentally aware. Simply hold this fierceness with love and kindness as well.

Thank your fierceness, thank your tenderness. Thank any resistance that came up as much as you give thanks for any breakthroughs or insights you might realize. Programming yourself with new beliefs takes the same kind of focus and repetition that has held the old ones in place.

End the meditation by sitting in silence and holding yourself gently. Let this become a practice that you do even for just two minutes a day until that peaceful, loving place within you is always there to go to whenever life gets hard. The more we visit these places, the more accessible they become.

{ **15** }

Reset.

The following exercise helps to break the mind free of rigid, habitual, or looping patterns of thought. Whenever you feel stuck in your head, this is a good way to invite a clear state of mind.

Chidaksha is a Sanskrit term that means inner space or space of consciousness— with this practice, we aim to clear the screen of the mind, eyes, and breath to have more clarity in that inner space.

Rub your palms together to create some energy and heat. Hold the palms gently over the eyes, with no pressure on the eyeballs, just around the eye socket. Take a few deep breaths and witness the black screen of the mind, maybe with some light or little swimmy things moving around on it. Possibly there are images with associated thoughts present. Press gently into the palms and "wipe" the screen clear as you move the hands over the eyes and out to the sides of the head a few times with long exhales as you sweep...

Next, open your eyes and turn your head to the right as you turn your eyes to the left, inhale as you turn, and exhale as you return to the center. Repeat to the other side. Do at least 3 to each side. Move with your breath.

Sex, Sexuality & Gender

A re Different Things.

> *"Sex differences may be "natural" but gender differences have their source in culture."*
> —Ann Oakley, Gender Theory; Author of "Sex, Gender, & Society"

> *"Gender "is seen as 'the social, cultural, psychological constructs that are imposed upon ... biological differences."*
> —C. Worthman, 1995 Anthropological Review

Many people conflate sex, sexuality, and gender, yet they are distinct. A survey by Pew Research Center (2022) found that 42% of Americans still believe gender is strictly binary, even as 5% of young adults now identify outside the binary (e.g., non-binary or genderqueer). The Trevor Project reveals that LGBTQ+ youth face higher rates of suicide ideation due to societal pressures tied to misunderstanding these distinctions. Dismantling these constructs can reduce stigma and save lives.

As we explore the specific binary of gender, our language needs to be aligned. Words have power. Take a moment to review these words and write down what comes up for you. Audit your past relationships with these words and where you are with them now.

- **Sex**: Technically refers to your chromosomes and genitals. Yet, it is not that simple. There are actually 40 variations of sex chromosomes and organs[8]. Traditionally, modern beings are lumped into being either assumed male at birth (AMAB) or assumed female at birth (AFAB). Despite it being inaccurate to their biology, intersex people often have one of these two labels put on them. 1 in 1500 to 1 in 2000 people are born with genitals that are not distinctly male or female[9].
- **Sexual orientation**: Who you are drawn to romantically or sexually. These could be the same or different for different folx. Asexual people can still fall in love and have a particular orientation.
- **Sexuality**: Your capacity for sexual feelings, sexual thoughts, and behaviors.
- **Gender Identity** is how one identifies with socially constructed ideas of what gender is or is expected to be expressed as. Gender markers and definitions can change throughout time, space, cultures, and generations. Gen-

der is not fixed. It is enacted, taught, and conditioned. Many people are born with sex and gender that matches expectations, and many are not but have been forced to conform, at least to some extent, without choice.

The way that our overarching culture views sex and gender is harmful to all of us. It limits and inhibits us. Sex and gender have in the modern world, traditionally been regarded as binary categories, leaving a painful, unidentified middle ground excluded. Here are some terms that we can use to refer to and become more familiar with regarding folks of the in-between. Continue your inventory and see what comes up for you when you review these words.

- **Cis**: Latin for 'on the same side as'. This refers to when your biological sex and assigned gender align. For example, someone born with a vulva who identifies as a woman.
- **Trans**: Latin for 'across from'. This means that the sex assigned to you at birth and your gender are 'across' from each other. For some, this may be a bridging or spanning - a 'here to there' kind of across, or it might be like 2 poles. Not all trans people take hormones or have surgeries. It doesn't mean that they are, as often experienced and stereotyped, "born in the wrong body". It is about the internal sense of across-ness—across the spectrum, this *and* that, not necessarily this *or* that. Although some may transition their gender or sex entirely, many do not. A trans woman, for example, identifies

and relates to the qualities that the given culture has ascribed to as "woman" despite being assigned male at birth and all of the expectations that come with that.

- **Gender non-conforming**: Your dress, tone of voice, gestures, etc, run counter to the expectations of your assigned sex. This can also refer to how the time and place you are born into expects you to behave. Women who wear pants or men who have long hair are past examples of gender non-conforming.

- **Gender Queer, Gender Fluid, Non-binary/Enby**: A person or description of a person who does not subscribe to conventional gender distinctions but rather identifies with neither, both, or somewhere in-between. These folx identify beyond the binary. This includes many 'two-spirit' identifications.

- **Intersex**: The definition from Planned Parenthood is "a person who is born with a combination of male and female biological traits. There are several different intersex conditions." These characteristics can include genitals, hormones, chromosomes, or reproductive organs. Intersex people can have a variety of bodies and gender identities and may identify as male, female, intersex, trans or non-binary, or something else. Up to 1.7% of the population is intersex.

- **Two-Spirit:** "Two-spirit" is the modern, generally accepted English blanket term for gay and trans native people. It cannot be translated into the Indigenous languages as, in many cases, it means something different.

- **Queer:** These days, the label "queer" can be used to describe all gender, sexual, and romantic minorities. It is a generally accepted term, although not all people in these identities and relationships accept or enjoy the phrase. The enforced gender binary creates the cultural ostracization of these groups. If there were not a decreed gender binary, it would not be 'queer' (as per the original definition of queer as "odd") to have anyone in the 'in-between.'
- **They:** Writers and speakers often use "he or she" when referring to an unknown individual. I frequently edit this to "they," as it's been used for a singular unknown person for a long time and is much more inclusive. My plea to authors and speakers: just use "they." It flows better and is more welcoming since it can refer to anyone.

Language changes. Sometimes, words can be used one way and then another. It can cause confusion when language changes. Women have long had to edit as they go, over lifetimes of reading books that referred only to "he" and "man" when they meant humankind or all beings.

There is a great Ted Talk by Sociolinguist Archie Crowley that can help us learn to accept new identifying language. In the talk, they point out that "Thou" was, in the 1600s, a term used for a singular person and "You" for a *group* of people. When "You" began to be used for a singular person, there was a lot of resistance, uproar, and offense.

Does that sound familiar? "They/them" has historically been (and still is) used to refer to a single person, as in, "Someone came by, and they left this," or "I heard someone outside but I didn't see them." We are reclaiming and evolving the use of "they/them/theirs" as pronouns for those who don't identify within the he/she binary or as pronouns for those whose gender we do not know.

Pronouns and grammar change over time. Language is alive, and as our language grows, it adapts to our ever-evolving needs. Growth and evolution are natural for all living things. Think of how many new words or new uses of words we have adopted in relation to our technological growth!

Review the following key points and make some notes in your journal about how they make you feel. Are you upset? Do you feel validated? The following points have been hot topics in my conversations around gender.

- The goal here is not to discredit or deny the existence of opposites. Opposing forces and opposite ends of spectrums exist. Men and women are constructs that are unlikely to disappear, though their definitions will continue to evolve. This work is about expanding our awareness of what else is possible and uncovering what has been hidden or suppressed.
- Women have long fought for their freedoms and equality, and this work continues as women are still not treated with the same respect as men in many situa-

tions. Women exist and are essential to our existence. As we shift our perspective on gender, the question arises: does one have to be a womb-bearer to be a woman? Some are born without wombs, some have them removed for various reasons, and some women have different anatomy but fulfill many of the same roles as womb-bearers in their culture. As a womb-bearer myself, I know we are raised and face risks differently than most people born with phalluses. Having experienced trauma and prejudice related to my female body—through menstruation, sexual violations, pregnancy, and birth—I believe womb-bearers (current or past) need their own safe spaces to gather, heal, and commiserate. Those of us advancing awareness around gender constructs are not trying to erase women or dismiss the unique challenges faced by those assigned female at birth. This is another area where language needs to evolve.

There are ways to be more inclusive while also creating spaces specifically for populations with shared experiences. Once again, this emphasizes the importance of our communication skills and using language that connects rather than alienates. I do not claim to have all the answers, and even as we reach collective agreements, there will always be those who hold differing views.

"Gender identity is a form of self-defini-tion...with which we can, to a limited degree, manipulate desire...Perhaps the more impor-tance a culture places on desire, the more con-flated become the concepts of sex and gender."

From Kate Bornstein in *"Gender Outlaw, On Men, Women & the Rest of Us"*

{ 17 }

Sacred Masculine & Sacred Feminine

You may have heard the terms "sacred masculine" or "sacred feminine". These terms were born out of a desire to reclaim the sacred, yet too often, they carry the misguided mindset of male and female attached to prescribed gender roles. In this binary, the sacred masculine is often depicted as the strong and assertive man (even though masculine does not mean man or male), while the sacred feminine is represented as the nurturing and receptive woman (feminine does not mean woman or female). This perpetuates expectations of how men and women are "supposed to be".

Personally, I want to be a strong, assertive, nurturing, receptive being who considers myself sacred and is treated as such. I believe that this is possible and *the birthright of each one of us.*

We are all made of many parts. Why assign them to sex or gender? So many qualities could be attributed to either or anywhere in between. We have experienced enough of the harm that this causes, i.e., "men" afraid to be seen as "soft" and, therefore, acting out in overly hard/machismo ways to prove that they are not. "Women" afraid to be seen as too aggressive, become people pleasers. We all have outward moving, powerful forces, and equally powerful receptive energies. We all exist in tender, fleshy bodies with sturdy bones. We all need and are able to provide care and protection. We are all composed of all of the elements. We all have weathers, seasons, moods, life phases, and energy cycles. Life cycles cause all qualities of being to shift and change in predominance within each of us. This can be over hours, days, weeks, months, years, or depending on our environment at any given moment. Our overarching culture tends to give these qualities disparate identifiers. But why polarize or gender them when we can be so much more specific and creative?

When many people hear the terms "sacred masculine" & "sacred feminine," they feel left out. Where do I belong? Do I have to choose only one to relate to? What do we actually *intend* to call in when invoking these sacred polarities? What *qualities* or aspects of being are we referring to when we use these labels? Let's specify the invitation and expand inclusion.

What do you mean when you are calling on your own or another's "sacred masculine" or "sacred feminine"? For example, often when people are calling in "sacred masculine," they are referring to a provider/protector archetype, but is this truly a masculine or gendered quality? What if we just called this "sacred protector" energy or "sacred provider" energy? Don't most beings play these roles? Do we mean outward-moving or inward-moving energy? What about using Sacred Solar energy or Sacred Lunar energy? Do we mean strength, resilience, sacred fire, sacred water, flowing energy, receptivity, action, mystery, radiance, expressiveness, groundedness, airy qualities...? Hone in, get creative. Play with naming specific qualities. They are all sacred in the right context.

Yin and yang are used in a similar way as masculine/feminine and are perhaps more effective when understood correctly. Yin and yang are inextricable from each other, which is partly indicated by the dot of the apparent opposite residing in the center of each. The way that the yin/yang symbol moves represents life force energy constantly moving, expanding, fading, contracting, dying, becoming the energy that feeds new growth, becoming new life, growing, revealing, concealing, a constant movement. They operate on the principle of enantiodromia: everything eventually turning into or making way for its opposite. There is no yin without the yang, as there is no Shakthi without Shiva, and we would not know Shiva without Shakthi. This is the same, Shiva and Shakthi are not separate and originally not gendered energies. They are representative of potential life, life coming into form, and dissolving back into pure potential. Shiva is the vibration of all things/pure potential, and Shakthi is that vibration coming into form—MA—mantra—words—physical form.

With attention to the radical/root meanings of these teachings and references, we become intimate with our wholeness and can engage with the fullness of our selves. Practice remembering yourself as the pure energy of consciousness/awareness that is beyond, beneath, within, and without the physical.

To deepen into the concepts of masculine and feminine, I encourage you to look at the work of Margaret Mead. She was one of the first to actively research the answers to questions regarding the relationship between one's biology and behavior around what we consider here in the West to be masculine or feminine. Mead traveled the world to discover that in many tribes and nations, men and women were both expected to behave in ways that we in the West had long been taught were "feminine". In many places both sexes were nurturing and took care of the children. Neither were expected to be aggressive. In some cultures the roles that Westerners have long assumed or stereotyped as masculine or feminine were reversed. For instance, she spent time in a society in New Guinea where females are the economic leaders, known to be the shrewd business people, and the males are the ones who spend a lot of their time "adorning themselves and gossiping"[10]. The Wodaabe, a nomadic African people, also have customs of male beauty pageantry and female sexual empowerment that are directly opposite of what we commonly know in the West.

Research on gender diversity around the world reveals expanded gender roles, multiple genders, obvious social constructions of gender roles, as well as constructed patterns of relationships around sex and gender. Like any construct, these are bound to collapse and change over time.

"Never doubt that a small group of thoughtful, committed individuals can change the world. In fact, it's the only thing that ever has."

—Margaret Mead, cultural anthropologist & author

"...

I guess I was forced into it.

I guess you might call the pornography a force

I guess you might call all the advertising a force

You might call the doctors who kept telling me

that if I wasn't a man, I had to be a woman,

you might call them a force.

You might call the fashion industry a force.

On the other hand,

you might call forcing someone to be one gender or another,

you might call that

a fashion."

...

"A viable solution to such a "choice" is to disentangle oneself long enough from the culture or individual presenting the two alternatives so that you can explore some other options"

—Kate Bornstein, author of *"Gender Outlaw"*

Journal Prompts:

- What do you actually mean when you say Masculine or Feminine?
- What might someone else mean that you wish they'd say?
- What might it mean for you to reclaim some aspect of sacred energy within yourself, no matter what gender you identify as?

{ 18 }

Questions From The
Audience Regarding Gender

When presenting this work in various settings, I have been asked some questions that I feel are important to include here.

"What about people with wombs?" This vague but important question arises in various contexts, particularly in discussions surrounding "TERFs" (Trans Exclusionary Radical Feminists). While I understand the fearful source of their angst, I do not condone their irrational and often hateful reactions to what they do not understand. Many AFAB individuals share similar concerns, wondering, "Where does that leave us, or what does it mean to be a woman?" Let's be clear: trans folks are not here to take anything away from people with wombs. It's undeniable that people with wombs have very unique experiences, such as having a menstrual cycle, the risks associated with pregnancy, and growing up with the oppressive teachings of femininity that have existed for so long. Being conditioned to be feminine and having a vulva or possessing a smaller, less physically overpowering body leaves many vulnerable to being overpowered. According to the National Sexual Violence Resource Center, 82% of AFAB individuals are sexually assaulted in their lifetime, while only 43% of men report experiencing the same. Trans individuals suffer from high rates of sexual violence, too, with estimates ranging from 50-66%, according to the National Coalition of Anti-Violence Programs. The rates are especially high for trans women, particularly for those of color. Thus, it is true that womb bearers and trans people need their own safe spaces to heal and process their experiences. It is also true that women can have penises and that some are born AMAB. "Woman" is a social construct with identifiers that can be seen naturally occurring in people of all sexes. Living as a woman has often meant enduring traumatizing and oppressively enforced expectations for people with vulvas. However, the concept of being a woman is increasingly becoming a choice as we begin to dispel the gender trance that has held us captive. What it means to be a woman is constantly changing and will continue to evolve as we fight for equal rights and freedom of expression and as styles of dress and gender presentations morph around the world.

Part of this inquiry involves our words. Discussing these considerations without allowing slander or hatred to creep in would serve communal harmony.

Consider these common questions and use them as starting points for conversations:

- Should there be different names for women with or without wombs?
- What about AFABs who have had their wombs extracted?
- Is "wombyn" acceptable to identify those with wombs or who have had them?
- Does "womxn" work to include all who identify as women, no matter what body parts they have?
- When should we differentiate between women and trans women?
- Will we, as a community, be able to evolve our language to work for everyone as we expand our understanding of gender?
- Can we see that much of the dissent stems from semantics?

There will be growing pains along the way. Be curious and have compassion.

"What about men?"—I want to acknowledge that this may be a challenging time for many men as so much of what you've been taught is being confronted and reexamined. It's clear that education around boys transitioning to men has not kept pace with the women's revolution across various fronts. Men's roles have remained relatively stagnant, often characterized as leaders, bosses, and figures of authority who are expected to be dominant, emotionally stoic, and resistant to vulnerability. We're all familiar with the classic portrayals of men—especially those of rich white men—that have shaped the behaviors of AMAB individuals for generations. However, this narrative is changing. Increasingly, we are witnessing strong and sensitive male role models alongside a growing acceptance of diverse cultural norms where men are encouraged to cry, show affection, express their needs, and ask for help. These are normal human expressions that boys have been unjustly disallowed or shamed for, for far too long.

"What about sex?" Or, more accurately, "What does dispelling gender mean about pairing up, attraction, and functioning sexually? What about the way that our parts fit together and the roles that we play?"

Our bodies fit together in many ways. As a teacher of partner yoga and a bit of a sexual scientist, it has been enjoyable over the years to play with the many ways that our bodies fit together and to marvel at the way that we are all built with a sacred geometry that lends itself to perfectly fitting *many* of our parts together in comfortable, strange, and exciting ways. So, to minimize bodies "fitting together" into PIV (penis in vagina) is quite reductive and way less fun than nature might have had in mind. Stay curious, experiment. We can all open ourselves to being attracted to people whose attitudes and physiques are beyond what we are pummeled with in advertising and media (which are the biggest perpetrators of binary conditioning on every level—gender, wellness, have/have-nots, in/out, etc.). Consider the possibility of realizing you have been blinded to some very exciting aspects of humans and your sexuality by this brainwashing.

A Personal Story: When I first got together with my love, Jess, they were in the first year of their physical transition. Before we became intimate, we talked about our desires and boundaries. Discussing what you like and want is sexy, even if it can feel uncomfortable at times. Jess expressed that they didn't want to play the expected role associated with being a penis bearer—initiator, dominant, and so forth. Instead, they wanted to embrace their feminine side, focusing on tenderness and receptivity.

In my excitement and giddiness of new love (even after all my queer years!) I enthusiastically said, "Okay, so I'll be the boy!?" But that was not what Jess meant. That moment exposed my own binary conditioning and ignorance. They clarified with all their grace and wisdom, "What I want is to learn together how Jess wants to be loved and how lucid wants to be loved."

Of course! It should have been obvious. I felt a bit foolish, and I couldn't help but laugh at my response to this beautiful request, which should ideally be the starting point for all intimate relationships.

I can't tell you how many times I've experienced partners conditioned by traditional male roles who then invariably acted out as inspired by scenes from porn, leaving me feeling disconnected. They weren't present with me; they were stuck in their heads about how sex was "supposed" to be performed. I, too, was a sex performer for a long time, and it seemed that most men wanted that dynamic, which gave me a lot of approval. Yet, despite my ego being stroked because I was a good performer, it was deeply unsatisfying to my soul. When I learned what it meant to truly connect with someone—experimenting with awe, reverence, and wonder at the divine being before me—sex transformed into something extraordinary that I had never seen on TV. It takes vulnerability to achieve real intimacy and touch the soul.

Dispelling our binary conditioning can be hot and sexy! I encourage you to experiment with giving yourself and your partner more freedom to express and explore in new ways outside of archaic gender expectations. (I could probably write a whole book on this topic alone!)

"How do I explain my gender to my family?" and "How do I put up with my family's ignorance and cruelty around who and how I am?" As you read this book and engage with the reflection exercises, I hope you gain valuable insights to help navigate these questions. You could start by explaining how sex and gender are different things. You might then follow by discussing the multiple genders of tribes and cultures of the world. Share some of their names and roles and discuss how they were, in many cases, violently wiped out or repressed by incoming colonizers. Tell them that you are alive at this time because it is a time of reclaiming what was lost to white supremacy and patriarchy. Ask them if they have ever been hurt by someone telling them that they are acting or look like the opposite gender. Ask them about how they felt about that. Inquire whether they think that was fair and if they want future generations to continue to feel that way. Truly meet them with curiosity, and as much as you can stay undefensive.

I want to acknowledge that many families will resist engaging in this dialogue or listening to your experiences without insults, shaming, or other negative responses. It's important to recognize that sometimes, we cannot change people's minds, and we may have to accept that some people choose to remain willfully ignorant.

While this can be a sad truth to accept, it's crucial to understand that there will be areas where we might need to surrender and focus on nurturing our own hearts and minds. Finding solace within a resonant and loving community can be a source of strength and healing during these challenging times.

Also, see "The Badass Spell" in the Spells & Rituals section at the back of this book.

> "Good leaders know there is no perfect solution. That is the lie and false promise of the dualistic mind, polarity, and all or nothing thinking."
> - Richard Rohr, in *The Naked Now*

{ 19 }

On Remembering

Historical References & Healing Modern Resistances

In the scope of history, it is a relatively new phenomenon to have only two options for gender expression. While the words we use may change, gender-expansive people have always existed. It is a timeless reality that humans present in a multidimensional array along a spectrum of what we call gender. We always have and always will. This section aims to help us place the present in a historical and cultural context.

How does a child know the history that has been kept out of their textbooks? How can a child who does not see people like themselves represented in popular culture even begin to imagine that the world once celebrated people like them and, in some places, still does? How can they know that they have the power to reshape the world into a place where they feel like they belong, just as they are? We begin by loving them as they are. Next, we teach them about our history. Sharing the truth of our often-hidden past is an act of love that helps prevent history from repeating itself. When we keep things hidden, it is usually due to shame. Holding onto shame and hiding the truth perpetuates the patterns that caused the unfortunate incidents. We dispel shame by honoring it through honesty. This allows us to move forward, seeing clearly and learning from our collective past. As adults who recognize the damage caused throughout history, we must confront our current violent and oppressive systems and structures. Change begins in our hearts, within our families, in our places of learning, in our communities, and in our laws.

"It doesn't really matter what a person decides to do, or how radically a person plays with gender. What matters, I think, is how aware a person is of the options. How sad for a person to be missing out on some expression of identity, just for not knowing there are options". — Kate Bornstein

For most of human history, we have recognized and even celebrated gender-expansive people. They are not "illegal". They are not trends or fabrications. Genitalia does not define a human's gender, individuality, or role in the world. A role might determine how someone dresses or acts, but it is not who they *are*. Let's share this knowledge, and each do our best to make our world safer and more informed for all beings.

Before Europeans colonized much of the planet, countless indigenous peoples acknowledged and celebrated multiple gender identities as a natural part of their culture. The process of colonization involved erasing what the invading culture disagreed with and assimilating the rest to facilitate the subjects' conversion.

"Research shows that more than 150 different pre-colonial Native American tribes acknowledged third genders in their communities."
— From a Human Rights Campaign article by Ana Flores, Nov. 2020

The British government instructed the invading colonizers of what we now call North America to erase all evidence of what we now refer to as two-spirit people. They received reports of "men" doing women's work and "women" dressing as men, which they deemed intolerable. Those individuals were forced to assimilate or face violent consequences, which, in some cases, included being thrown to the dogs or into mass burial pits. It is difficult to recount this past, but I do not want to sanitize history or diminish its tragic nature. This suppression is why most people today are unaware of the many-gendered history of the lands we occupy. The colonizers sought to maintain control over the people by taking away their language, spirituality, sacred lands, and various freedoms. The repression of gender expression was one of these means of control[11]. Now, we have the opportunity to rediscover our rich histories and reclaim our freedoms.

Many First Nations people acknowledged diversity in gender and sexual identity. In many tribes, children were dressed and treated the same until they displayed the characteristics pertinent to certain roles (which we now often ascribe to assigned gender). Then, they were offered the outfits and support befitting those roles.

Many tribes believed that a person who could see the world through multiple genders or perspectives was gifted by the Creator and deserved esteem. Gender-expansive individuals often served as medicine people, midwives, spiritual leaders, artists, craftspeople, teachers, and leaders within their tribes. These gender-fluid individuals were seen as capable of moving between earthly and spiritual realms. Their fluid nature was understood to grant them the ability to interact with spiritual dimensions. This worldview continues to be upheld by many cultures that honor their gender-expansive people today.

"In my culture we have people who dress half-man, half-woman. Winkte, we call them in our language. If you are Winkte, that is an honorable term and you are a special human being and among my nation and all Plains people, we consider you a teacher of our children and are proud of what and who you are."

- Native rights activist & American Indian Movement co-founder, Russell Means

Global Gender Names List

In the following list, I have mostly kept the language true to my sources, but I found that some terms were archaic or written from a binary gender-conditioned perspective. I have modified some terms (but never the names) where needed to align with our commitment to honoring gender diversity and to reflect the language we support moving forward.

When referring to someone born with an outwardly developed vulva or vagina, I have described them as AFAB (assigned female at birth). For those born with an outwardly developed penis or testes, they are described as AMAB (assigned male at birth). It's important to clarify that it is not necessarily their culture that assigns them as female or male, but rather how our current culture relates to the bodies they were born into. I use the term "outwardly developed" because, ultimately, we all have the same anatomical components in different configurations. Some individuals are born with what we would classify as female or male parts that are not outwardly evident, or they may not develop these parts until later in life. Sex and gender can change throughout a person's lifetime.

Some sources for this list highlight how entrenched we are in binary conditioning. For instance, some references describe a third gender as "encompassing both genders," implying that only two exist while attempting to create a third rather than recognizing a spectrum of more than two options. Again, I have tried to honor my sources while updating any insensitive or outdated language.

Here are *some* indigenous tribal names and descriptions for sex and gender-fluid members organized alphabetically by name, tribe, or location in the world.

Aboriginal Australia—Indigenous transgender people are known as "**sistergirls**" and "**brotherboys**". This is a modern term. Several Aboriginal nations have traditions of culturally specific gender categories. Some of the pre-colonial names are; "**Kwarte Kwarte**" in Arrernte, "**Kungka Kungka**" in Pitjantjatjara and Luritja, "**Yimpininni**" in Tiwi, and "**Karnta Pia**" in Warlpiri, which can be interpreted as "like a girl", while "**Kungka Wati**" in Pintipi and "**Girriji Kati**" in Waramungu literally mean "woman/man".

Acault—a third gender in Myanmar consists of males assuming women's dress and social roles, known in Burmese slang as Acault. Acaults often serve as spirit mediums in the indigenous animistic belief system. While some Acault are heterosexual, not all are.

Aravanis—of Tamil Nadu—A subset of the hijra tradition are the Aravanis, who are assigned male gender roles at birth but adopt female gender roles early in development. They take their name from the mythical deity Aravan.

Asegi—of the Cherokee/Aniyvwiya—Southeastern Woodlands, US—Asegi is a blanket term & variant term for different man/different woman. Male-assigned: **nudale asgaya**, Female-assigned: **nudale agehya**. In Cherokee, Asegi udanto refers to people who either fall outside of men's and women's roles or who mix men's and women's roles. Asegi, which translates as "strange," is also used by some Cherokees as a term similar to "queer."

Ashtime—of Ethiopia—Ashtime is a term used in Maale culture that describes an AMAB individual who dresses as a woman, performs feminine tasks, cares for their own houses, and apparently has sexual relations with men. This could be homosexual/homoromantic men, transgender women who are attracted to men, transfeminine non-binary individuals, or similar identities.

Baklâ, Bayot or Agî—of the Philippines—Bakla is a Tagalog term that encompasses an array of sexual and gender identities but especially indicates a male-assigned person who assumes the dress, mannerisms, and social roles of a woman. While bakla have existed as a recognized third gender for centuries, more conservative influences in recent decades have marginalized them.

Bote/Bate'/Bade—of the Crow/Apsaalooke— largely from the Yellowstone River Valley, US—*batée* is a word that describes both trans women and homosexual males, meaning "not man, not woman" (male assigned). *Bate'* is an AMAB person in a Crow community who takes part in some of the social and ceremonial roles usually filled by women in that culture.

Burrnesha—of Albania—aka Verginesha—First documented in the 1800s but traced back to the 1400s, Northern Albania's burrnesha—"sworn virgins" are AFABs who take a vow of chastity and wear male clothing in order to be viewed as men in the highly patriarchal society where women had little to no rights, including having no right to speak, whereas burrnesha were respected. The tradition exists to a smaller extent in Kosovo, Serbia, and Montenegro. The tradition is dying out: There are believed to be fewer than 50 sworn virgins left in the Balkans.

Chibados—of Central Africa, Ndongo and Matambo (modern-day Angola), Historically, the people of Africa largely considered biological sex to be an illusion. They knew that humanity and deity existed on a spectrum. In Central Africa, there were spiritual leaders called Chibados who were what we now call trans folx. They were believed to be diviners with superpowers and magical insight. Some gender spectrum deities from Africa are: Lansa/Oya—Orisha of the winds, a gender variant/masculine woman, Exu—a trickster God, gateway between earth and divine, gender-fluid, queer, and Osumare—gender variant deity of rainbows.

Chuckchi of Siberia (and neighboring Indigenous peoples, including the Koryak and the Kamchadal) are nomadic, shamanic people who embrace a third gender. Generally, shamans are assigned male roles, with some adoption of female roles and appearances. They married men but were not subject to the social limitations placed on women. Third-gender Chuckchi could accompany men on the hunt and take care of family.

Cree/Ininiwok, Canada—**Napêw Iskwêwisêhot**, man who dresses as woman, **inahpikasoht**, a woman dressed/living/accepted as a man.; "someone who fights everyone to prove they are the toughest." Male-assigned: **Ayahkwêw**—man accepted as woman, possibly not a respectful term; others have suggested it is a third gender designation, applied to both women *and* men, Female-assigned: **inahpikasoht**—woman accepted as man. **iskwêw ka-napêwayat**, "A woman who dresses as a man /One who acts/lives as a man.", **iskwêhkân**, "One who acts/ lives as a woman"

Egypt—Tai, Sht, Hmt—During the Mamluk Sultanate in what is now Egypt from the 1200s to the 1700s, young AFABs who were perceived to have masculine traits were celebrated and raised as boys and afforded all of the legal and societal advantages. Pottery shards from the Middle Kingdom of

Egypt (2000–1800 BCE) found near ancient Thebes (now Luxor, Egypt), list three human genders: **tai** (male), **sḫt** ("sekhet") and **hmt** (female). Shai/Shait was a genderfluid god/dess who would be referred to alternatingly with the name Shai, when female, and Shait, when male.

Fakaleiti—Similar to the third-gender traditions in Samoa and Hawaii, the Tongan fakaleiti, is an AMAB who adopts feminine dress, mannerisms, and social roles. They do not necessarily consider themselves to be transgender or gay, which are considered strictly Euro-American constructs that do not apply.

Femminiello (roughly "little man-woman") in Italy refers to AMABs who dress as women and assume feminine gender roles in Neopolitan society. Their station in society (up through the 19th century) was privileged, and the rituals (including marriage to one another) were based on Greek mythology related to Hermaphroditus and Teresias.

Geenumu gesallagee, (AMAB), meaning "he loves men," perhaps correctly spelled, ji'nmue'sm gesalatl are of the Mi'kmaq people—Northern Atlantic woodlands, North American continent.

Guevedoche—of the Dominican Republic—genetics seems to have created a third sex in the Dominican Republic. A heritable pseudo-hermaphroditic trait was discovered by ethnographers in the 1970s who followed the children over generations. With undifferentiated genitalia, they generally were raised as girls but began developing male traits at puberty. Instead of changing their gender identities to male, most chose to live as a third gender called guevedoche (roughly meaning "testicles at 12") or machiembra (man-woman). The society has accommodated the guevedoche and constructed a third gender with distinct roles for them.

He'ema—meaning 'woman-man', indicating a singular effeminate AMAB, He'emane'o is plural. (hee = "woman", hetan = "man"). **Hetaneman**, indicating singular masculine AFAB, meaning 'man-woman', Hatane'mane'o (plural). Of the Cheyenne people, territory once ranging from what we know to be Montana to Texas, including parts of Oklahoma.

Heemaneh—of the Cheyenne/Tsitsistas of the Great Lakes Region, US, pushed into what we now know as the Dakotas and Nebraska. Heemaneh is a cross-gender or third-gender person, typically AMAB people, who take on the roles and duties of a woman. *Heemaneh* have had specialized roles within Cheyenne society, including officiating during the Scalp Dance, organizing marriages, acting as messengers between lovers, and accompanying men to war.

Hijira—In South Asian cultures, including India, Pakistan, and Bangladesh, hijras are AMABs who adopt feminine gender identity, women's clothing, and other feminine gender roles. In the past, the term referred to eunuchs or those born intersex or with indeterminate genitalia. Most hijra do not consider themselves to be men or women or transgender, but a distinct third gender.

Intersex—Intersex is a Western term for a third sex, and some intersex people consider their gender to be intersex or **non-binary**. Intersex people are born with sex characteristics that do not fit typical binary notions of male or female bodies. Intersex is an umbrella term used to describe a wide range of natural bodily variations. In some cases, intersex traits are visible at birth, while in others, they are not apparent until puberty or may not be physically apparent at all, and variations could be in reproductive organs, chromosomes, or hormones. Since the 1950's, the medical establishment has been non-consensually conducting surgeries to "normalize" these children. 1.7% of humans have an intersex trait. Human Rights Watch and Pidgeon Pagonis, an Intersex activist, have teamed up to convince hospitals to stop this automatic procedure and help ensure bodily autonomy and acceptance for intersex children.

Iran—There is evidence of third genders existing in civilizations in the region that is now Iran dating back thousands of years, but that is generally not acknowledged today and it is a hostile place for trans folx. Transsexual rights are limited but acknowledged in Iran, where it is still punishable by death to be gay. Due to a decree by Ayatollah Khomeini, gay and/or transgender men are permitted to live lives as straight women if they undergo sex reassignment surgery, after which their official documents are changed to reflect their new identities.

Kathoey—Thailand—Very loosely translated as "ladyboys" (which today is seen as a slur). Thailand's third gender kathoeys are known as being born assigned male but "having a female heart," according to a common Thai saying. They are often referred to as sao praphet song or a second type of woman, some prefer simply sao which means woman. Thai tradition holds that true kathoeys are neither male nor female but inhabit the space between binary genders.

Köçek of the Ottoman Empire—From the 17th through the 19th centuries, the Köçek were a cultural phenomenon in which young AMABs dressed in women's attire and formed traveling dance troupes that performed sexually suggestive dances. Today Köçek culture in Turkey survives as a folkloric dance tradition.

Lakota (Teton Sioux)—**Winkte'** means "feminine male", and **bloka egla wa ke** is the term for Two-Spirited people "born female, lives as man". Historically in the Upper Mississippi River area, the US, forced into the Great Plains.

Lhamana—of the Zuni two-spirit tradition in which a person lives as both genders simultaneously. They play a key role in society as mediators, priests, and artists and perform both traditional women's work (pottery and crafts) as well as traditional men's work (hunting).

Machi of Chile, Mapuche (earth people), are considered religious authorities capable of balancing the Mapuche cosmos.

The Machi's gender is determined by their identity and spirituality, not by the sex assigned at birth. This fluidity of gender is what allows them to interact with the spiritual realm.

Māhū—of Hawaii—meaning "those who embody both", can also mean 'in-between' or, 'gender fluid', a traditional third gender from Native Hawaiian culture. Historically, māhū were assigned male at birth (AMAB), but in modern usage, māhū can refer to a variety of genders and sexual orientations. In pre-American Hawai'i, māhū were notable priests, healers, and teachers, usually of hula dance and chant. Since the term māhū can have multiple spaces and experiences, the terms were adjusted by Wong-Kalu, a renowned mahu, and split into four new words;

Ha'awahine is a term used for AMAB people who are emotionally, spiritually, psychologically, and culturally female. If they have begun dressing femininely and/or physically transitioned (through HRT or surgery), the term **Ho'owahine** is used instead.

Ha'akane is a term used for AFAB people who are emotionally, spiritually, psychologically, and culturally male. If they have begun dressing masculinely and/or physically transitioned (through HRT or surgery), the term **Ho'okane** is used instead.

Mashoga is a Swahili term in Kenya, Tanzania that connotes a range of identities on a gender continuum. While loosely used to indicate gay men, a large proportion of mashoga are AMABs who adopt feminine gender early in life.

They characteristically wear both men's and women's clothing, but in a manner distinct to mashoga alone. They often assume female roles and serve a crucial role in wedding ceremonies.

Maori culture has **Wakawahine** as men who prefer the company of women and take up traditionally feminine occupations such as weaving. **Wakatane** denotes an assigned female who pursues traditionally male roles, such as becoming a warrior or engaging in physical labor.

Meti is an indigenous term for a third gender in Nepal, with a long history in the Himalayan region. They are born assigned male but assume feminine dress and carriage.

Mino—of Benin/The Kingdom of Dahomey (now Benin) had an all-female regiment of female warriors called the Mino (our mothers). They were unmarried and childless women who were thought to have masculine or aggressive traits.

Mixu-ga of the Osage/Wazhazhe—Midwestern/Great Plains, US—meaning "instructed by the moon", an all-encompassing third gender.

Mojave/Aha Makhav—Colorado River/ Mojave Desert, US—the creation myth of the Mojave tribe speaks to a time when humans were not sexually or gender-differentiated. They recognize four genders: men, women, **hwame** (male-identified AFABs), and **alyha** (female-identified AMABs).

Muxe is a recognized third gender among the Zapotec people in Oaxaca, Mexico. A large population of Muxes has been celebrated since pre-colonial times. Muxes are part of the culture and its traditions.

Napumsaka—of India—is a non-binary third gender throughout time and currently. India also has deities that represent the fullness of a human being, being both male & female. Besides Siva/Sakti, who are usually shown individually but are indeed one, there is Ardhanariswara, represented as half/half, male/female. India's Supreme Court, in 2014, ruled that "it is the right of every human being to choose their gender" and now officially recognizes those who do not identify as male or female as transgender, as a third gender. At this point, there are an estimated 2 million transgender people in India.

Navajo/Dine'—Southwestern, US—**Na'dleehi** = "one who is transformed/one who changes/one who is in a constant state of change"—refers to a traditional third gender, including intersex, in which an AMAB person embodies both the masculine and feminine spirit. **Dilbaa** refers to an AFAB person with a more masculine spirit. Both are considered to encompass male & female in one person.

Ninauposkitzipxpe—of the North Peigan tribe of the Blackfoot Confederacy in northern Montana and Southern Alberta, Canada. /*ninauh-oskitsi-pahpyaki*, roughly translates as "Manly-hearted-woman." This term has a wide variety of meanings ranging from women who performed the roles of men, dressed as men, took female partners, or participated in activities such as war. Honored as a third gender, they were AFAB who did not necessarily dress in a masculine mode but were unrestricted by the social constraints placed on women in the Blackfoot society.

Ojibwe/Anishinaabe—have a gender-neutral language with many words to describe various expressions of sex and gender, including unique words for ages and actions. Here are some: **Ikwe'**—Female, **Inini**—Male, **Indigokwe**—like a woman, **Indigonini**—like a man, **DagoKwewi**—woman spirit within man, **Dag-Ininiwi**—man spirit within a woman, **Ikwe-waadizi**—has the nature of a woman, **Ininiiwaadizi**—has the nature of a man, **Ikwekonye**—dress like a woman, **Ininikonye**— dress like a man, **Ininiikaazo**—women who function as men, **Ikwekaazo**—men who function as women.

Ojibwe/Chippewa—North American/Subarctic—**Agokwa or Agokwe**, meaning "man-woman," Female-assigned—Okitc-itakwe, meaning "warrior woman."

Onnagata or Oyama in Japan—since the 17th century, these are the names for males who have trained, often since childhood, to embody female characteristics and play female roles in kabuki, traditional Japanese theater. These people were often chosen because they exhibited feminine qualities. The practice of males playing female roles arose when women were banned from the theater.

Paiute—Great Basin, US—**Tuvasa** (Northern) AMAB, & **Tudayapi** (Southern) AMAB: **Tuwasawuts**—both meaning "dress like other sex."

Peru—Inca, In pre-colonial Andean culture, the Incas worshiped the Chuqui Chinchay, a dual-gender god. Third-gender ritual attendants or shamans performed sacred rituals to honor this god. The **quariwarmi** shamans wore androgynous clothing as "a visible sign of a third space" that negotiated between the masculine and the feminine, the present and the past, the living and the dead. Their shamanic presence invoked the androgynous creative force often represented in Andean mythology.

Samoa—Polynesia— four assignations/genders—M/F, and **Fa'afafine & Fa'afatama**—fluid gender roles that move between male & female worlds.

Sekrata people of Madagascar who have male sexual characteristics, but after displaying behavior viewed as feminine during childhood, they are raised as girls. *Sekrata* adopt a feminine appearance in styling their hair and wearing jewelry. As adults, they inhabit a unique niche, often performing in ceremonies. The *sekrata* are widely accepted within Sakalava society. They are viewed as both sacred and protected by supernatural powers.

Sipiniq—Inuit/Inuktitut—Arctic Regions of North American continent—usually for a female assigned infant, whose "sex changes at birth". Sipi, meaning "to split". The idea is that a newborn infant might have been perceived as having male genitalia that "split" to become female genitalia. This infant would go forth as a man in society, performing male duties while having female genitalia. This can be considered a third gender, or in modern society, as an example of transgenderism. They were also considered very spiritual and were prime candidates for the shaman role.

South Sulawesi, Indonesia—The Bugis have words for five genders that map onto five ways of being in the world. They recognize three sexes (male, female, intersex) and five genders: men, women, **Calabai, Calalai, and Bissu**. Calabai are assigned males who embody a feminine gender identity. Calalai are assigned females who embody a male gender identity. Bissu are considered a "transcendent gender," either encompassing all genders or none at all.

Travesti—In some cultures of South America, a travesti is a person who was assigned male at birth, has a feminine gender identity and is primarily sexually attracted to non-feminine men. Travesti's feminine identity includes dress, language, social, and sexual roles. Many describe themselves as homosexual. Travestis may modify their bodies with hormones or silicone but rarely seek genital surgery.

Uganda—Prior to colonization, the Ankole people in what is now Uganda elected a woman to dress as a man and thereby become an oracle to the god Mukasa, acting as a bridge for the people to the divine.

Waria—of Indonesia—a term used for the third gender, includes individuals who identify as male but behave as women, perhaps wearing makeup and women's clothing. Others identify so closely as female that they are accepted as female in society.

Xanith of Oman are considered an intermediate gender in this Islamic nation. They are assigned males who assume the dress, mannerisms, and some social roles of women. Under Islamic law, they have all the rights of a man, many of which are denied to women.

Zuni—AMAB: Lha'mana, meaning "behave like a woman" AFAB: Katotse, meaning, "boy-girl."

& From the Talmud—the 8 Historical Jewish Genders—

1. *Zachar*, male.
2. *Nekevah*, female.
3. *Androgynos*, having both male and female characteristics.
4. *Tumtum*, lacking sexual characteristics.
5. *Aylonit hamah*, identified female at birth and later naturally developing male characteristics.
6. *Aylonit adam*, identified female at birth and later developing male characteristics through human intervention.

7. ***Saris hamah***, identified male at birth and later naturally developing female characteristics.
8. ***Saris adam***, identified male at birth and later developing female characteristics through human intervention.

"In fact, not only did the rabbis recognize six genders that were neither male nor female, they had a tradition that the first human being was both. Versions of this midrash are found throughout rabbinic literature, including in the Talmud." (from MyJewishLearning.com)

There are so many references to expansive gender in our history that creating an exhaustive list is impossible. I welcome your additions for future edits.

> " ..*For thousands of years Cultures from Siberia to West Africa have words for third sex people, or other genders who embodied both masculine and feminine*"
> — Hannah Fons, Master in Sexuality & Gender studies, non-binary trans-person & activist

We no longer have access to many of the stories and names of the in-between beings of indigenous tribes as the histories were destroyed and the people taught shame, their lives threatened if they carried on their traditions under colonial rule.

"The (original) peoples of North America ... saw no threat in homosexuality or gender variance. Indeed, they believed individuals with these traits made unique contributions to their communities". —Roscoe, from *"Changing Ones"*

So many of the early accounts and ensuing research about Indigenous gender variance are misleading as it is written by white European men who filtered what they witnessed through their narrow understanding of gender. In addition, they largely ignored the female experience. They used inadequate and now offensive terms such as homosexual (when that was not the case), transvestite, hermaphrodite, etc. When gender variance was later communicated, it often referred to *alternate* genders when it was largely *not* the case that native tribes saw these as 'alternates' but simply as one of the many ways of being.

Sex and gender have been conflated in many dominant societies, yet they are distinct concepts. Sex refers to the genitals a person is born with, while gender is a social construct that refers to the roles one plays in their culture. This conflation has caused gender policing, which we have all experienced in some form. This may have initially come from the expectations of authority figures but has extended to communities and families policing of behavior and presentation, causing authoritative correction, violence, feelings of rejection, depression, and other negative outcomes.

We disconnect from our true selves when we are taught that our feelings or expressions are wrong. This disconnection puts our emotional stability and overall wellness at risk, which can ultimately affect the health of our families and communities.

What if we made more space for the wide variety of ways that life expresses itself? Access to our diverse histories provides us with a different lens to perceive ourselves and the world. With this knowledge, we may not feel that something is wrong with us. This leads to healthier, more realistic self-concepts and, consequently, happier, more stable individuals.

Feminine expressions of gender have changed rapidly over the past few generations. From fighting for the right to vote and no longer being considered the property of men, to wearing pants, working outside the home, and advocating for equal pay, women have made significant progress and continue to fight for equal treatment with men. Creating systems and structures of equality is one way to reconstruct gender. We can reject the unjust and divisive norms handed down to us. So, why should we accept the constructed binary that suggests there are only two genders? The story that any individual should act in a particular way or fulfill a specific role based on their genitals is entirely manufactured.

I am grateful to see that, at least in the circles I am fortunate to be part of, what were previously considered "feminine" expressions of gender are now more widely recognized and encouraged in both males and females. Historically, we have witnessed that oppressing these traits has been unnatural and harmful, and we have all suffered because of it.

Our overarching culture, especially in the West, and many of us individually, have been under the spell of what gender is "supposed to look like" for so long that we may not even know what gender can look like because it has been hidden from us. However, we can re-imagine, feel, and live into it.

SELF-INQUIRY

- What might it look like to not have societal gender dictates?
- What gender expectations are you personally ready to move beyond?
- Can you celebrate yourself and others expressing as you/they are, not as the labels historically and harmfully imposed upon us all?
- We may find ourselves having identity crises around gender identity. What if we also took that opportunity to look and see that gender and identity themselves are constructs that we can choose to believe in or not?

{ **21** }

Dance Break!

It's time to get out of your head and into your body. Enjoy laughing at the silliness of gender and imagine the freedom you might experience by recognizing or dismantling these constructs. It may seem contradictory to affirm the construct by acting it out, but remember: We are just playing. We are playing for a cause.

Play is crucial for our healing and for understanding of who and what we are! This exercise (along with the Nona Fender's Angels & Demons exercise in the back of the book) uses play in the form of what you might call "camp" or burlesque. Originally, burlesque was intended to make fun of the serious issues of the time, long before it became primarily associated with striptease. Burlesque is "an absurd or comically exaggerated imitation of something, especially in literary or dramatic work; a parody."[13]

In theater and film, camp is a style and performance identifier that largely originates within queer communities. It employs exaggeration and theatrical devices to deceive the audience temporarily. Camp can also involve the playful reappropriation of clichés, tropes, or outdated elements such as gender. Drag and burlesque performances magnify "real" life and draw attention to cultural phenomena that might otherwise be overlooked or overwhelming without humor and play. So, lets play...

Instructions: Put on some fun, uptempo, sexy music, and give these cues with 30 seconds or so between them. Exaggerate the qualities of each cue. Be silly! It can help to go big into what we are trying to dispel to see it more clearly and laugh at the ridiculousness of these constructs.

1. *Dance like a "man"!*
2. *Dance like a "woman"!*
3. *Dance the in-between!*
4. *Dance like a "good" person*
5. *Dance like a "bad" person.*
6. *Dance like you are free of labels!*
7. *Dance like fire! Water! Air! Earth! Mud! Steam!*
8. *Dance the all and everything!*

"Camp can be a leading edge in the deconstruction of gender, because camp wrests social control from the hands of the fanatics. Camp in fact reclaims gender and re-shapes it as a consensual game. Setting about to do away with gender could itself turn into a frighteningly fanatical mission. Fanatics are distinguishable

by the fact that they can't laugh at themselves. Camp is the safety valve that can keep any gender activism from being fanaticism.

In doing away with a bi-polar gender system, one needn't do away with playing at genders. Drag is fun!"

— Kate Bornstein, *Gender Outlaw*

{ 22 }

Return to Beginner's Mind

Beginner's Mind is a concept rooted in Zen Buddhism. It emphasizes approaching experiences as if you're a beginner, with curiosity, openness, eagerness, and a lack of preconceived ideas. This mindset allows you to see the world without the constraints of your past knowledge or experiences.

Journal Prompts and Conversation Starters

Approach these questions without any expectations. Consider details you might normally overlook. Allow yourself to explore ideas without immediately needing to answer "Why?" and "What if?" Cultivate curiosity and openness.

- *What might it look like to return to a beginner's mind on gender?*
- *What else could gender look like?*
- *What are some ways that you have been exploring your own expressions of gender?*
- *What/Who inspires you in the world as you look at the possibilities of gender expression?*

- *Notice when your thinking is affected by cultural conditioning —is this what you would choose to think in regards to yourself or another?*
- *Notice how you identify and how you vary in ways of being and feeling that could be called more 'masculine' or 'feminine', and so on, with all the ways of being. Are you ever all one way or another?*
- *What is it to just feel human?*
- *All gender expressions are ever-changing. What if we did not habitually gender-limit anyone?*

Knowing & Healing Through Unity

In the following sections of this book, I aim to provide re- sources to solutions, inspirations, and new perspectives to help you explore ways to dispel the binary conditioning that may have negatively impacted your life.

> **"The curious paradox is that when I accept myself just as I am, then I can change."**
> **- Carl Rogers**

One of the most powerful tools I've discovered for healing and self-awareness is the multi-faceted gift of yoga. Yoga is an expansive philosophy and system encompassing a multitude of practices for wellness and awakening. It's important to clarify that yoga doesn't solely refer to asana or the physical prac- tices commonly associated with it; that is just one aspect of the journey if you choose to explore self-knowledge along the yogic path. The practices of yoga include breath work, movement, meditation, sound, and mindfulness, and are designed to help us consciously connect with and unify the various layers of our being. Yoga philosophy teaches us not to be defined by our thoughts or beliefs. Humans often identify with these constructs and become ensnared in them, suffering from them and even engaging in conflict or war over them.

We achieve union with ourselves and the source of life when we stop identifying with our thoughts and remember our essence beyond the confines of the mind. The practices of yoga are designed to help us know the Self beyond this busy mental activity. True understanding arises when we rest in pure awareness, revealing our fundamental nature as peace, joy, bliss, love, and interconnectedness.

This realization has been a common thread throughout history, as individuals engaged in spiritual work, meditation, or psychedelic journeys often arrive at, or at least glimpse, this expansive state of being.

Both yogic and Buddhist teachings hold that falsely identifying with the mind, thoughts, and ego is a primary cause of suffering. The entire practice of yoga originated as a way to see beyond the torturous impulses, thoughts, and emotions to consciously realize the expansive nature of our true Self.

In Yoga, we are invited to work with the bodymind (not two different things) in order to know ourselves as spirit having an embodied experience. I interchangeably use the words spirit, essence, nature, pure awareness, divine, and consciousness. Please use what feels right for you. All of these are words or phrases that attempt to describe the Oneness that we all are, a Oneness that manifests as multiplicity. You might have other words.

When we identify with our thoughts and feelings, saying things like, "I am sad" or "I am disconnected," we create suffering. Try experimenting with different phrasing: instead of saying "I am sad," try saying "I am *feeling* sad," or instead of "I am disconnected," say "I am experiencing a sense of disconnection." Yoga teaches us through direct experience that when we recognize pure awareness as our nature, then we find peace and spaciousness both within ourselves and in our surroundings. We are consciousness *experiencing* our feelings; we are not our feelings.

The Yoga Sutras of Patanjali, written in 500 BCE, are thought to distill teachings previously only handed down verbally. They offer a path to awakening laid out in 196 aphorisms, or sutras. In this context, Awakening refers to remembering ourselves beyond the body, beyond form or identity, even as we navigate what it is to live an embodied life.

Yoga Sutras 2-4:
2. Yoga is to still the patterning of consciousness
3. Then Pure Awareness can abide by its very nature
4. Otherwise, awareness takes itself to be the patterns of consciousness[14]

These three aphorisms are the foundational premise of classical yoga. They outline what the following sutras and practices go on to illustrate: that we suffer identification with our patterns of consciousness and reach bliss, connection, and awakening when we remember who we truly are: pure awareness. These practices for awakening to our essential truth have been developed for centuries.

The teachings and practices of yoga are vast and varied, as reflected in the many texts and styles available. I have been studying and practicing yoga for over three decades, and it has played an integral role in my healing and self-discovery. I continue to learn and thrive due to the practices of yoga. I have been sharing these practices with others for nearly as long and continue to have them celebrated and affirmed as crucial healing tools through my work with others in general and directly therapeutic sessions.

Healing through unity requires recognizing our interconnectedness in one way or another. There are many ways. Here, I champion yoga. In all of the practices of yoga (asana, breath, meditation, chanting), we come together as an intentional community. Studies show that these kinds of strong social support systems reduce the risk of mental health crises by up to 40%, according to the World Health Organization (WHO). Community-based healing practices, like group therapy and mindfulness, have been proven to lower cortisol levels (a marker of stress) and increase feelings of belonging, as documented in a Harvard study on resilience in 2021. These findings underscore the power of connection in overcoming division and reaffirm the ages-old wisdom of yoga philosophy and practice. I encourage you to meet your fellow yogins. Yogic communities have been such a blessing in my life and the lives of those around me.

{ 24 }

Remembering the Unity In Our Diversity

*f*rom a Tantrik perspective

"I searched for myself & found only God, I searched for God & found only myself"
—Rumi

In Yogic and Buddhist philosophy, there are three primary causes of suffering, known as the malas. A mala is an impurity of thought, often described as a "stain" or "cloak" on our awareness. Awareness of the malas is said to help us grow, but ignorance of them causes suffering.

The first mala is Anava mala or ignorance. The other malas are rooted in this one. Anava mala refers to the ego's ignorance of our interconnected, divine nature, this ignorance keeps us feeling small and separate.

In the yogic view, "I AM" means, "I am that (all that!), I am at one with the divine, I am all that I experience through the senses, I am the divine/universe experiencing itself through these senses". When facing Anava mala, the ego-mind tends to think that "I AM" means being separate from all else. Ignorance as a "stain" speaks to this tendency. The ignorance of the *existence* of these obscurations causes misalignment with reality. Either way, the focus is ignorance, not knowing (or forgetting) that we are all inextricably connected to earth and to spirit. This ignorance causes heartache and feelings of unworthiness.

The next two malas arise from this feeling of separation. Mayiya Mala is suffering of the mind, which causes jealousy, grasping, hoarding, theft, and other behaviors we would not enact if we knew ourselves to be whole and connected. Karma Mala is suffering related to the body, causing fear of death, worry, and feelings of self-worth attached to worldly accomplishments.

When we are consumed by our "I"-ness, we suffer the pain of this perceived separation. The pain of separation leads to fear of the perceived "other," blame, greed, attachment, avoidance, clinging, loss of the will to live, and fear of death. This worldview of separation leads us to harm each other and the planet because we do not readily see or feel our interconnectedness. This ignorance keeps us from experiencing freedom and liberation in our lives, individually and collectively.

Awareness of the malas can help us dispel the binaries of us/them, in/out, this/not that, and others, including life/death and the human habits of grasping or clinging for fear of not having or being enough. Witnessing these patterns of consciousness and depersonalizing them without identifying with them can dispel them. It is a practice in itself and can be part of a mindful meditation practice.

The spiritual teachings of yoga, especially Non-Dual Tantrik Saivism (personal bias, please investigate for yourself), help us to see clearly again, to remember who we truly are, and awaken us to our connected divine Self. These teachings are not unique. They are inherent in all religions but have been obscured by dogma. On my personal journey, Non-Dual Tantrik Saivism has been my guide. Some engage with it as a religion. Yet, It is also a philosophical system that doesn't require religious adherence. The teachings are offered to aid in making sense and ease of life, free of the strings and constraints so often imposed by religion.

> *"All sentient beings, seen and unseen, are simply different forms of one divine consciousness. Each of us is a vantage point within one all-encompassing and unbroken field of awareness."*
> From *"Tantra Illuminated"* by Christopher Hareesh Wallis

The philosophies of Non-dual Tantra invite us to re-cognize the nature of consciousness in such a way that each of us can, through empowered, informed reflection, come to realize our own true nature. However, there is no proof of this true nature other than our individual internal process and awakening to it. This can happen in moments, in pulsations, and sometimes all at once through meditation, spiritual practice, or study. For some, it manifests as a peak moment, such as those delivering shaktipat— a sudden spiritual awakening, especially as evoked through the blessing of an "enlightened one" or guru. Please investigate for yourself. The path will unfold differently for everyone and for each of us at different times. Part of this investigation of self is to play with all that it is to be human. Engage with activities and identities that help you to learn. Discover new parts of yourself without notions of sin or supposed to be's.

From 'Essence of the Tantras' by Abinivagupta, Kashmiri philosopher, circa 1000 CE: *"This whole universe is One Reality—unbroken by time, uncircumscribed by space, unclouded by attributes, unconfined by forms, inexpressible by words, and impossible to understand by the ordinary means of knowledge"*

In this worldview, each human being is unconfined, universal consciousness having an embodied experience. We are all of it *and* are restricted in our comprehension and explanations by our limited perceptions. Words can only point to the truth or *part* of the truth. There is so much that we cannot see, hear, or sense that exists. There are many ways of knowing. This is what the dynamic system of yoga practices is for. In the spaciousness and relative silence of meditative practices, inexplicable truths can arise as knowing. In the movement and forms of asana, we may get glimpses of lesser-known aspects of ourselves and release identifications or limitations that are no longer serving our growth and well-being.

As humans, we tend to believe our thoughts and define ourselves and our lives by them. We view life through an inherited lens of rigid assumptions. We tend to think these stories that we tell ourselves, called *vikalpas* in Sanskrit, *are* reality itself, but they are incomplete representations that may have served a particular need for a limited time. The archaic definitions of man/woman and good/bad cause us suffering. It is taught that vikalpas are the only cause of suffering. You are detaching from your wholeness when you tell yourself or believe someone telling you that you have to be 'this or that'. You fracture the self and set yourself up for suffering. Instead, have fun playing with possibilities and be aware of forming rigid identities or becoming attached to certain ways of being.

Tantrik philosophy understands thought as another sense, like sight or sound. Thoughts are impressions that spontaneously arise in the field of awareness without our effort. *Thinking*, on the other hand, is what we *do* with these thoughts. The mind is like a radio receiver. Sometimes, the broadcasts are unclear or don't tell the truth; often, they are re-runs. You can choose to think in new ways and tune into a new station. We learn through practice how to discern which thoughts actually require attention and how to change the channel to avoid those that don't.

The ability to recognize our vikalpas, or mental constructs, as *representations* of reality and not reality itself is said to be the most crucial skill of a Tantrika. It is from questioning reality that we grow nearer to knowing it. We must take time to be curious about our individual senses, emotions, and thoughts and *ask questions* of ourselves. All of our relationships will benefit from this approach. *Stay curious and ask questions* before you judge or try to define anyone, including yourself. *This* is dispelling binary thinking and the artificial constructs that have been laid before us, which keep us divided.

We get to choose which perspectives to take. Ask yourself, are your current perspectives healing or harming? Emotions and thoughts can spin stories that seem like truth, but they can cause us to lose sight of the big picture. The practices of tantra, yoga, meditation, and mindfulness help us slow down and feel what human things must be felt. They open us to the big picture. Through them, we learn to sense the vast, infinite, divine, connected consciousness that We All Are.

I offer this brief overview of non-dual Saivism to examine how mental constructs restrict us and how to heal that. We have agency in what we think, how we show up, and how we treat others and our shared world. We have the power to create new realities. Each of us has this ability. Together, we are even more powerful.

{ 25 }

Attention & Intention

I have met many members of modern healing communities who claim to be "into tantra" or identify as Tantrikas. Yet, I have been shocked at the lack of accurate information taught at the neo-tantra classes I have attended at various festivals and community spaces over the last few decades. Most alarming is how much binary programming is being reinforced.

Anthropomorphization combined with patriarchy has distorted the teachings of tantra and many spiritual paths. Shiva/God is not a man or male but the essential vibration of consciousness/awareness that constitutes all things. Shakti/Goddess is not a woman or female, but the energetic principle of vibration/consciousness coming into form. Shakthi is an inextricable part of Shiva, without whom we couldn't know Shiva. In essence, neither of them is gendered or has a face. Humans have nonetheless given them faces and pronouns, as this is how we view the world. There are countless global stories of the divine as (a) multifaceted being(s), where "they" represent non-gendered energies that either make up or create all things, depending on interpretations. In many of these related teachings, all is one, expressing itself as many. These nuances can be found in various esoteric religious writings, which were later simplified and commodified for the masses, creating power-over structures that took power from the people.

Most people who intend to be healers or who identify as counselors, therapists, or coaches are well-intentioned and genuinely want to help others. Yet, despite their best efforts, they still struggle to fully live up to their ideals. After all, we're all humans on a journey, navigating and unraveling layers of conditioning along the way.

Here is one recent example:

I met a woman at a festival who identified as a Relationship Therapist. She was serving guests at the tea temple, a space where anyone could come for free tea served by rotating volunteers. While addressing the group, she frequently used "guys" and occasionally "ladies." Since this was a conscious, multi-gendered community that values mindful language, she twice corrected herself, acknowledging that her language was not fully inclusive but habitual.

Afterward, she spent about five minutes (maybe longer—I left to avoid schooling her in front of everyone) complaining about how difficult it is to change language. She remarked, "It's just so hard to rewire and stop saying 'ladies and gentlemen' when you've been doing it your whole life."

This is true. I empathize—and *this is the problem!* Even those who have dedicated their lives to relationship care can struggle, or sometimes outright refuse, to slow down, be mindful, and be fully present. They miss the opportunity to offer care through their words and the impact those words have.

Yes, it's hard. It requires practice, patience, persistence, and compassion—for oneself and others. It calls for a genuine willingness to grow in ways that support the well-being of everyone involved, including ourselves.

But isn't that what we're here for?

This is what meditation and mindfulness are for—to help us break free from habitual, reactive patterns and engage in the hard work of change. They teach us to be present with all that transformation requires. And it *is* worth it. Your own freedom and the well-being of those around you are at stake.

We shape the world with our attention and our words.

I don't claim to be perfect or "better than" anyone. I stumble, I do the work, I stumble again, and I keep going.

Understanding our relationship with ourselves, our world, and all beings is required if we are to show up with integrity. It takes effort to resist conforming to the status quo and to take time to think, reflect, and challenge the constructs we've inherited. The very things that cause us to struggle can become our greatest gifts when we shift our attitude or perspective. As the saying goes, *"Growth lies just outside the comfort zone."*

Mindfulness means watching our mind, attending to our thoughts, and noticing the subtleties of our experience and the ways that the self operates. It is about being present with what *is*, moment to moment. It is a life-giving, life-saving practice. With practice, mindfulness becomes a way of life that provides us with endless growth opportunities. Mindfulness enables us to expand our center of steadiness and peace. Mindfulness eventually gives itself to a state of ease within an open, non-judgmental, yet keenly insightful and intuitive awareness.

When we can be at ease in our energy body, our physical body follows suit. The rigidity of body and mind, fear, and judgment melt away. Our natural joy, curiosity, and awe of life have more room to delight in the world. From this place we can approach our problems with creativity.

{ 26 }

Intention, Impact & Fucking Up

#1 *Rule—don't make others do the work for you!*

As you move forward in watching what you are perpetuating with your language you may stumble or feel resistance on your path. The most important thing I can tell you is *it's ok to fuck up.* You *will* misspeak. You *will* misgender people. Notice when you make an assumption, repeat an old joke, or use an archaic reference about gender, race, performance, embodiment, or other characteristics. Do not make a big deal about it. Notice, acknowledge, apologize, and carry on. When you stop and overly express sorrow, guilt, shame or try to explain yourself by way of your own personal stories, then you are making it about *you.* You are making the other person do the work of then trying to make you feel better. Don't beat yourself up. But more importantly, don't make others do the work to make you feel better when you get something wrong.

Find your own resources to process your feelings around getting it wrong. Do this with other allies, *not* with the person who you may have (unintentionally) slighted. They are not your resource. Do the work on your own time.

Practice saying this phrase:

"I apologize for using the wrong pronouns. I realize that my words may have hurt. I've got work to do, and I'm going to do it."

Here's an example of what *not* to say:

"Oh my god, I'm so sorry, I feel so bad, I totally wasn't thinking, I'm so used to... I just...(personal stories). I'm really trying to... but my, my... I, I...

Sharing your pain, your story and your excuses can make the person you may have offended feel like *they* need to take care of *you*. This is disrespectful and exhausting, and it deepens the offense. Instead, I suggest that you apologize, correct yourself, and move on.

MICROAGGRESSIONS -

Sometimes, in our attempt to make connections with those who are different from us, we falter. We make thoughtless comments, including words intended as compliments. These remarks can reveal our ignorance, hidden biases, -phobias, or -isms. For example, attempting to flatter by saying, "You're the most beautiful trans person I have ever seen," is deeply harmful. Sadly, this was said to my beloved at a festival. A comment like this fails to see the person in front of you as a unique individual. True care involves being present. It is to see each being in the moment. Notice your thoughts, and ask yourself what you really want to express before speaking, even if your words are meant as a compliment.

Would you say, *"You are the most beautiful Black person,"* *"You are the most beautiful redhead,"* or *"You are the most beautiful grandmother"*? Do you hear how discriminatory that sounds—as though the type of person you are referring to is not typically or not expected to be beautiful? This subtly implies that their identity is an exception, rather than seeing their beauty as inherent and not tied to a label.

The examples above are called *microaggression*s. This is a term that refers to remarks made in ignorance, without intent to hurt the other. It is not your intent but the *impact* of the words that matters. Usually, those who commit microaggressions are unaware of the impact of their words or actions. People may use their intention as an excuse for the impact they have, but regardless of intent, mindlessness—or something that might be dismissed as a minor or "micro" comment—can still be deeply wounding.

The term *microaggression* was coined in the early 1970s by Dr. Chester M. Pierce, a medical doctor and professor of psychiatry at Harvard University. It was used to describe subtle common behavior and communication that is dismissive and insulting to Black people. These behaviors can have traumatic effects and impact the physical and mental health of those receiving the (unintended) offense. People can receive microaggressions as part of any marginalized group. The definition has been clarified and expanded by Dr. Hsu, who defines three types:

1. Microassaults, which are more intentional

2. Micro insults, which are more subtle, verbal, and non-verbal. For example,

telling a person of color or immigrant that their English is very good.

3. Micro-invalidations. For example, repeatedly using the wrong pronouns.

To be in integrity, you must take responsibility for your *impact*. Please be aware that we all have an unconscious, implicit bias in many areas of life despite what we might consciously think. These biases are based on our early life and even pre-verbal experiences or understandings, including what we learned from others that we might consciously object to. We can have preconceptions about people based on their appearance that we don't even realize are affecting our behavior towards them.

GO DEEPER—

When asking a question or giving a compliment, question what it is that you really want to communicate? What is the essence and intention of what you are trying to express or ask? Are you trying to connect? What is the authentic expression of your truth in this desire? Be sure that your approach is free of judgment or expectation. See each person as an individual, not as a representative of a group or type. Stay curious. How might this person be affected by your query? Remember, you are not entitled to know anything about another person that they do not choose to share with you. Do not ask someone what is in their pants, what they were *born as*, or where they are from based on their accent or skin color. Do not ask what their *real* name is. Anything someone shares with you about themselves is a gift.

We are always constructing our reality and, therefore, always have the opportunity to deconstruct expired norms. All of our thoughts, words, tone, intentions, and choices make a difference.

The following is paraphrased from a Language Alchemy®[15] podcast by Alejandra Siroka , referencing the work of Dr. Diane Goodman:

How to respond to microaggressions—*for receivers or witnesses*

- Don't say anything? Are you in danger if you respond? Talk to someone trusted later. (Discern in the moment which of these is best.)
- Plan to communicate skillfully later instead of reacting in the moment.
- Be prepared w/micro-interventions—strategies to confront w/ready statements.
- (if you receive microaggression) Ask for clarification or more information, ie; "what exactly did you mean by that?"
- Separate the person's intention from the impact. Remember, the person is usually not aware of their impact and does not intend to hurt you. They are behaving with implicit bias. Tell the person what their impact was.

- (if you witness microaggressions) Challenge the stereotype! Give information, share your own experience, offer alternative perspectives.
- Share your own process, what you heard, and what you learned in relation to what was said.
- Promote Empathy - ask how they would feel if someone said something like that about their friend, partner, or child.

And,

Here is a personal view with some push-back on the term "Micro-Aggressions" from Reverend Lien, a wonderful, non-binary Buddhist teacher whom I have had the blessing of co-teaching with. It is important, as we address nuance and language, to receive these perspectives;

"...While I understand that "microaggression" was formulated to describe subtle racism, the definitions themselves minimize the targeted person' experience, focusing on an evaluation of the physical impacts when the psychological and emotional impacts are reduced or ignored. Such a definition doesn't account for the responsibility of the one doing the speech or action; that it's from the same hate-driven motivation whether it's conscious or unconscious, covert or overt.

It's the impact of hate-driven motivations which we need to heal from. While racism affects us all, it's BIMPOC who feel hatred's malicious force the most.

Be safe. Be safety to all."
- Rev. Liên, she/they[16]

Of course, the point is that although we might call something a micro-aggression, it does not feel micro to the person receiving it. So, they invite us to look a little deeper at what is happening.

{ 27 }

Language Awareness

Make an active practice in your life to update your language to be more inclusive. Instead of habitually using phrases that continue to divide us, try shifting your language to be an outward expression of your respect and understanding. When you make a mistake, just correct yourself. It won't take long for new habits to form. Here is a list of commonly used phrases and some non-gendered counterparts for you to practice:

Instead of...	Try this:
Ladies and Gentlemen	Humans, kin, gentlefolk, distinguished guests, friends, beloveds, fellow travelers
God/Goddess	Good forces, creator, dei'i, source, spirit, holy being, Go-den, Divine, sacred beings
Priest/Priestess	Priestex, holy one, spiritual guide, wise one
he/she (unknown gender)	they/them, this one, that one, or use a person's name
tranny	transgender, transperson
Masculine/Feminine	Use the specific qualities that you are referring to
father/mother	parent, guardian
husband/wife	spouse, partner
son/daughter	child, kid, offspring
brother/sister	sibling
boyfriend/girlfriend	person, partner, significant other, sweetie
you guys	y'all, everyone, folks/x, kin/dred

Please note: you can also search for more extensive lists online including updated names for professional roles.

"Communication is like partner dancing," says our friend Jane Arc, *"you're gonna step on some toes and fuck up. Don't stop and make a big deal out of it.. just keep dancing"*

{ 28 }

To Be A Good Ally

To begin with, let's acknowledge that to be a good ally to anyone is to love ourselves. When rules, limitations, and judgments are placed on anyone, we are all subject to them. We inhibit our freedom to be who we are when we deny the freedom of others to be who they are. Ideally, we stay curious about who we are, as life is about change. If we are living fully, then we are constantly changing. Stagnancy = death. To stay curious and compassionate with who you are and who others are is to be the greatest ally in all fights for liberation and freedom.

With that said, here are some key points of attention when looking to connect with others:

- Ask for pronouns; do not assume. Default to *they/them* if you aren't sure. Respect individuals' pronouns.
- Don't make a big deal out of getting it wrong. Apologize, correct yourself, and move on.
- Don't assume anyone's gender or ask about their *gender journey* without being in a consensual space.

- Avoid using gendered language, and aim to use gender neutral language when addressing groups.
- Never touch anyone without permission.
- Have no expectations of what someone can/can't do or might want.
- Do not express your opinion about someone's gender, pronouns, or bathroom choices.
- Give support to people questioning their gender or place in the world.
- Never ask someone what is in their pants.
- Never ask what they were born as, their birth name, or assigned sex.
- Never ask where someone is from based on name, accent, or skin color.
- Never ask for any other name besides that which is shared with you.
- Remember to see people as individuals and not representatives of a group.
- Ask for consent before taking anyone's photo.
- Focus on complimenting things that the other person can control, such as their style, personality, or accomplishments.
- Avoid commenting on people's bodies or ask for consent first.

If you have ever felt held down, ignored, threatened, or inhibited by societal norms and dared to make the more difficult choice—the one authentic to you—then you are a world changer. When you summon the courage to be in your integrity and choose what is true to you, you inspire, welcome, and give permission for others to do the same, thereby creating a culture of love and connection.

This work is about cultural definitions, expectations, and how our words can limit or expand our expressions of self. Using our words carelessly, inwardly or outwardly, causes cognitive dissonance and fractured minds. It can lead to depression, anxiety, self-harm, dependencies, and the passing on of abuse to others. When someone is not loved for who they are, it is hard to love others for who they are. Love is the answer, after all.

When encountering someone who thinks differently than you or who is shaming/ making fun of someone that you want to be an ally for, ask these questions of yourself and them:

- What do you want to understand about this person/ these people?
- What do you want them to understand about you?
- Why is this personally important to you?
- What life experiences have shaped your views?

"The gifts of acceptance in the face of excruciating vulnerability..."
—Ali Hannon

"Conformity requires us to minimize our differences for the greater good. We fear that if we don't conform, we will be abandoned, but there is no loneliness like having people only see you after you have erased yourself"

- ALOK Void-Menon, *Beyond the Gender Binary*

TRY THIS!

A Little Improv Game for Ice-Breaking & Connection Events:

SAME - NOT - SAME

This could be used as a fun way to connect to someone at a party when you don't know what else to say, or it could be used as a get-to-know-you conversation starter for a dinner party or event. The name of this game makes it easy to remember how it goes! You simply ask each person to share one thing that they think they likely have in common with the other or with the whole group, and one thing that they likely do no have in common with anyone else playing the game. Usually there will be surprises! Leave room for others to relate, share stories, entertain, and be entertained! It is not just about the question but the revelations and unique points of connections that arise with any new person or group. You can continue on with each person taking multiple turns as often people get more open and inspired to take risks after witnessing others.

Love Is Attention

Love is remembering our connection. Love is lifting the veils of perceived separation with curiosity, awe, wonder, and reverence. Love is opening to the fullness of life itself and the myriad ways that it comes into form.

ATTENTION = LOVE
Giving attention to something or someone is an act of love.

REFLECT:

- What are you giving your attention to?
- Are you giving it with intention?
- What could use more of your caring attention?

I encourage you to turn this practice of attending to your attention into a regular meditation. When we slow down with intention we notice things we might not have seen otherwise. Notice how the attitude that you bring to a situation can affect both your experience and the response of the person or circumstance involved. When we bring our caring attention to something or someone, we find connection. We learn new parts of ourselves. When we take time to connect, we recognize all of life as one shining, multi-dimensional pattern of wonderfulness.

Love is the visceral experience of our shared being-ness. We find the oneness that we are in consciousness. Our natural state is love. When our shared being becomes eclipsed by the content of thoughts, then we forget the love and connection. *All that separates and forms hatred between beings are thoughts.*

True love is paying attention to our minds. This is the way that we can change the world. To live in a world of love and connection happens by getting to know our minds. By observing our thoughts and where our attention is going, we notice when there are thoughts or beliefs that are causing separation and fear. Engaging with fear takes us out of being present with what *is* in the moment. Noticing and naming fear and the sensations it creates in the bodymind can bring us back to the present and help to dispel fear. This is an everyday practice. Being present is the greatest gift of all.

We all have some unconscious bias based on our conditioning and life experiences. Mindful observation of our automatic thoughts, words, and actions can reveal these biases to our conscious selves.

Having grown up in a multi-racial and multi-gendered family, I thought I had no biases around race or gender. I was wrong. With hindsight, I can see how my conditioning failed me. My beloved partner, Jess, noted once that I called lots of my female friends, including those who are not mothers, "mama." Casually, I would say, "What's up, mama?" But, she observed that I never called *her* mama—my Jess, the greatest mama of them all. In hindsight, I can see the unconscious bias. Jess was non-binary, AMAB, and yet she was in so many ways more what our society considers a *woman* or *mama* than many of my female friends. She was a mothering force in her work, personal relationships, and communities. I regret my blind spots and sorely miss having her wisdom and presence as I complete this book that she inspired so much of. I continue to learn from her as I attend to this work.

I know these questions might come up:

Is it necessary to do all this work?

Do we have to work so hard to change our minds and habits?

Do we have to pay so much attention to our thoughts and words?

So I respond:

What else is there that we have power over which can instantly affect our experience of reality?

This is the journey. This is life.

As we change ourselves, we change the world.

Meditation—How's the Body?

Take a moment to attend to your body after delving so deeply into the mind. Read the following steps as a guided meditation, pause between each step, and allow yourself to be taken on a journey:

Become aware of your body.

Become aware of the natural movement of your breath.

Notice where you are holding any unnecessary tension.

Let anything you notice be interesting and not a judgment.

Become present with any thoughts or feelings that are active or humming in the background right now.

Consider if these thoughts or feelings are affecting your breath and body.

Return your awareness to the breath. Imagine letting the exhale melt away any judgments or stories.

Rest in the space that your intentional breath creates...

Practice this awareness regularly, and when you encounter challenging situations, it will become easier to return to yourself and resist acting impulsively. It's wise to avoid making major decisions or comments from an activated, stressed-out state.

Instead, use mindfulness as a tool to slow down and explore what else might be possible. How else could this situation be viewed or discussed? Recognize the quick surge of reactivity, but also tune into the quieter presence of nuance and possibility.

The more we practice checking in with ourselves, the easier and more familiar it becomes—like any place we visit regularly. Over time, this habit creates a sense of spaciousness around our emotions and the physical responses they trigger.

In that space, we gain the ability to respond intentionally rather than reacting out of habit. We can choose to breathe, pause, and focus on words and thoughts that foster connection rather than defensiveness or division.

Yes, just slowing down and attending to ourselves can make our lives easier and the world a better place.

In the spaciousness of silence and stillness, the knowing beyond words arises.

{ 30 }

Living In the Liminal

It's hard to be non-binary in a binary culture. After the death of my beloved Jess, it was heartbreaking to find in their journal how deeply they questioned their non-binary identity. They knew it was who they were, but they did not feel safe in what they perceived to be an increasingly hostile world for trans folx.

Many enby/non-binary folx and trans people suffer daily fear of the violent acts perpetrated on people like them. They experience the immediate challenges of not having a safe bathroom option, constant misgendering, being called either sir or ma'am when they are neither, and a barrage of other microaggressions. These latter concerns may seem trivial in the threat of physical violence, but they add up to living in a constant state of trauma and can affect all levels of health and well-being.

Queer and marginalized folx of all sorts have often been taught that something is wrong with them and, thereby, have been taught directly or indirectly to hate themselves. To dispel these early life beliefs requires vigilance. It takes honoring to dispel the shame one carries regarding self-deprecating constructs of mind. Honoring those of the in-between must include creating safer, more inclusive spaces. Allowing the evolution of language to acknowledge and embrace those who have been outside the artificially created margins is a crucial step in creating a more inclusive culture. Only together can we expand the current culture to include those who have been excluded. In this way, we all are safer, richer with love and support, to be the fullness of what we are.

In a recent dialogue with an acquaintance, I was told that they thought non-binary identity was a fad. This person said people were "claiming to be non-binary" and asked, "How can so many people suddenly be realizing that they are non-binary?'"

My response was this: many people are only just waking up to the fact that it's an option. The truth of our multi-gendered histories has been largely eradicated. These people may have wondered for years, "Where do I fit in? What is 'wrong' with me?" or "Am I gay?" or "Do I need to get surgery to change my sex or appearance to be accepted?". Only now are they realizing that there *is* a home for them, in their bodies, in this world, as they are. The problem is *not* the people awakening to options. The problem is the sick, oppressive, limiting structures and systems that we have all been stuck in. We must release the antiquated, habitual language and be open to the full spectrum of possibilities to grow and expand beyond these old, limiting constructs.

People do not have to change their bodies through surgery or hormones to be accepted or to be trans. We have the technology, and people have been changing their bodies for all kinds of reasons for generations. If this is something that you are considering, then please do your research and talk to those who have had these procedures. Some of these things are irreversible and have consequences that are important to know. Experience varies vastly. Some folx see it as counter-intuitive to try and match social expectations of gender when their goal is to liberate themselves from expectations. Others finally feel at home in their body with the support of medical interventions. It's your choice whether you pursue medical support or just change your clothing, hair, makeup, name, voice, or any way of carrying or presenting yourself. If you don't ascribe to the cisgender binary, then you don't have to. As with all things, there is a spectrum of ways to be a woman, man, trans, non-binary, gender fluid, or gender non-conforming. These gender expressions are available to all, irrespective of assigned sex or genitals. I have witnessed my loves experiencing both euphoria and regret in turns about their decisions, as most of us do in turns about our haircut, home purchase, or partner choices. I have chosen to remain the dynamic, multifaceted, undefined being that I am. Such is life: we experiment, we make choices, we learn, we grow, we change.

Living in the liminal, the in-between, the ambivalent, ambiguous, androgynous, neither-here-nor-there space can be quite challenging. Yet, as we have discussed, most everything in the universe exists on a spectrum. It takes more effort to un-

derstand the nuance rather than check a definitive box. Most
things are, at their essence, unknown and unnameable. Life is
largely beyond our control, like the weather, incidents, and ac-
cidents. We have always lived in uncertainty. Anything can
happen at any time. Yet, we have been taught to believe that
we are, or should be, only this or that: girl/boy, gay/straight,
good/bad, black/white, in love or not in love. We have all suffered from these dichotomies. We were led to believe that we
had to make a decision, pick one, check the box, and move forward. This belief is limiting.

It can be uncomfortable to live in the undefined middle. It
can be challenging for those around us. When living in the in-
between without a clear label or box to check, the simple act
of using a public restroom can become a challenge. Yet, spectrums, dimensions, constellations, layers, and shades of being
exist in all aspects of life. We are busting out of the boxes.
In different situations, days, decades, or company, we are different, and that's ok. We can even thrive in this. We are all
beings of multiple origins, viewpoints, identities, and much
more. Thriving in the in-between, in uncertainty, acknowledging our lack of control or clarity, taking risks, living fully in
expansiveness, shedding all labels, and dancing with the mystery is all possible—this is where the magick is! I propose that
the more courageous, more life-full-juicy-rich place to be *is*
dancing *in the middle*! As we practice allowing more spaciousness into our lives, we discover more creativity and, therefore,
more possibilities.

The culture at large is steadily moving towards reclaiming
wider ranges of acceptable self-expression, broader, more in-

clusive worldviews, and once again embracing multiple genders. Unfortunately, there is a conservative backlash happening, but the conversations are open as they have not been for generations. People are beginning to openly acknowledge and embrace intersex people rather than ignore them or force them to choose or change their sex or gender to conform to a mandated binary, thanks to Pidgeon Pagonis and other activists on this front. Very slowly, there are options appearing on many forms with check boxes for those who do not identify as solely male or female, woman or man. We will keep moving forward in this reclaiming.

How do we celebrate the unknown or undefined when our nervous systems want to feel safe and secure, and we still have public systems that do not see beyond the binary? We attune to ourselves and to our needs; we seek safety, comfort, and knowing in the support of community, tribe, and chosen family. As humans, we naturally seek identification and acceptance from those around us. We want to know what to expect, where we belong, what to call ourselves. This is the animal part of our human nature, how these human organisms are wired to survive. Our most primal fear, of course, is death. Once upon a time, we might have died without the support of our tribal family. So, when we are rejected for being different, it can strike this primal fear and leave us feeling that our lives are in danger. Befriending our nervous systems, working to understand what's happening, and practicing grounding and presence can support the re-wiring of these reactive habits. All aspects of yoga, meditation, and mindfulness can be crucial supports in this.

In many ways, we are all dealing with a heightened fear of the unknown as our world changes so rapidly. Environmental, social, and political systems, as we've known them, are in upheaval, and familiar paradigms are falling away. It is scary for most humans as our animal bodies like familiarity. How do we find ease with the unfamiliar and unknown? It is a practice or many practices. Repetition is key. Practice seeing yourself and how it is natural for you to change or want to change, and how you suffer not changing. Notice how people tend to connect their fears to their political choices and *other* people that they aren't familiar with. We can find more joy in life when we open to the mystery in every situation and allow more diversity of experience and expression.

Binary thinking has been taught to us since our first thick cardboard books, where we learned words. Up/down, in/out, girl/boy, happy/sad. I have never seen a kid's book that taught: on the way, in-between, half this, half that, a little bit of this, and the next moment that. The closest may be Dr. Suess' "My Many Colored Days", which acknowledges that some days we feel one color and others, another. We could use more media that acknowledges the rainbows of all our beings!

Nature can also teach and heal us. If we pay attention to nature, we find countless creatures who are outside human definitions of the norm. For example, there are many creatures who can change their color or sex as needed for survival. There are many creatures who form lifetime bonds, some with the opposite sex and many with the same sex. There are animals who do not pair bond, some who are polyamorous, and some who transition from one kind of creature to another, such as a caterpillar to a butterfly. In between is the gooey part, the imaginal part, where the magic happens.

We can all continue to understand more complex concepts, nuance, and how to see things from multiple perspectives. So, we continue to grow and change. We create safer spaces and art that helps us all to see beyond the binary, to learn about each other and ourselves. We use new words and references to frame and comprehend our experiences. As we mature, life offers us chances to remember our mortality, our divine nature, and the ever-expanding realms of consciousness and possibility. Taking a wide view of life and staying curious is the medicine. From this perspective, there is much wonder and permission to behold. We can see how narrowly humans have defined many things to try and make life feel less scary via the illusion of control. But life will keep moving and changing, as that is the nature of energy and life. Therefore, we effort to practice expanding our perspectives to live in and co-create a more joyful and loving world for all.

Here are some words that evoke the in-between; liminal, ambivalent, ambiguous, amorphous, androgynous, invert, betwixt, mixed, queer, fluid, medial, intermediary, interpolated, threshold, transitional, transitory, transformative, transmutation, agender, nuanced, expansive, inclusive, dialectical,...

Take a moment to savor each one, and maybe look up any that are new to you. How can attention to new words support the reframing of your place in life?

There will always be binary or contrasting experiences in life. Dualism is part of non-duality! Let's pause on the last word I mentioned above: dialectical. This is what we are calling in— dialectical thinking. We are not trying to do away with all opposites but to dissolve being held under the trance of believing we are supposed to be only one thing or another. No one is the boxes that they are forced to check. We all have facets, stories, and complexities that do not fit in the boxes. I know this can get mind-gym-like, but this work encourages you and others to blossom into fullness by dissolving artificial, limiting constructs and rigid identities. In other words, this book is about dispelling all-or-nothing, black-or-white, dichotomous (the opposite of dialectical) thinking. We too often see dichotomous language, hyperbole, and divisive language on the news, campaign ads, and social media. This is because dramatic, sensational, reductionist perspectives stir up emotional responses. Instead, a dialectical approach offers a more open, nuanced, considerate, and expansive way of thinking. Dialectical thinking seeks to harmonize opposing viewpoints. It is open to options and opposites. It reminds us that every situation has what we might call positive *and* negative ingredients, most often in ways that are inextricable from each other and feed one another like yin/yang, day/night, and life/death.

Dialectical Thinking Exercise

This is a Tantrik as well as a psychological exercise.

Use the prompts below to reflect on situations, identities, or beliefs that you have. Write out ideas or stories inspired by the questions and statements below;

- "I am (this)" and/or "I am not (that)"
- "I always (do this)" or "I would never (do that)"
- "You (or that person) make(s) me/This situation makes me..."

Bearing in mind the statements above, ask yourself the following questions:

- Are any of these statements or situations absolutely true?
- What *else* is true or could be true?
- Are you *also* the opposite?
- Are you sometimes *both*?
- What other points of view *could* you have?

Some examples;

"I always tell the truth."—But wait, is that true? Did you just tell a lie or a partial truth? We all sometimes leave out facts, avoid saying things, soften versions of the truth, tell a *white lie* so as not to upset anyone. When it comes to *truth* or other important values, extreme words like *always* and *never* are usually inaccurate. Truth is often subjective and deserves more nuanced attention.

"He makes me so mad."—You feel angry regarding a particular individual, which is understandable; it happens. But is it their behavior, what they represent to you or remind you of, or do they trigger feelings of sadness or fear that might cause anger to come up as a defense? Did they *cause* this anger, or is it how you heard something or how you wish things to be different that is causing anger? Could you change how you are listening and what you are focusing on, and thereby change how you feel? Is there space for compassion or empathy for that person? Can you see beyond their behavior or words to what they are trying to express or access in this situation? Can they make you angry and cause you to feel other things? Are your *preferences* causing the unwanted emotion?

"I am human!"—Well, obviously you are so it seems hard to argue with, yet, are you also spirit? Are you an animal? What is this *"I"* you speak of !? Even this seemingly straightforward statement has nuance to discuss.

Bring your attention back to the moment. How does it feel to look at situations in your life in these more nuanced ways? Could you make this a practice?

Resources are available and growing for us all to become less divided in our thinking, language, and, therefore, behavior. As we do this work for ourselves and expand our awareness and understanding of those who are different from what we have known, our empathy and compassion grow, and the world becomes a safer place for *all* beings!

I hope that works like this help people find home more fully in their bodies and this world. Even if it is a fad for some, so many things are. We all get to try things on: What if I'm a punk? What if I'm a jock? What if I'm a slut? What if I'm asexual? What if I'm an artist? Or a business person? An irreverent reverend? A sacred prostitute? A wild spiritual teacher? A humble leader? What if I had bigger breasts, or no breasts, or long hair, or no hair? We get to try these things on if we want to. Let no one tell us what we can do with the bodies we were born into unless our actions would harm someone else!

What if you are not what you were told you were? What if YOU GET TO PLAY WITH INFINITE POSSIBILITIES in this lifetime!?

You can. Have fun with it! We are divine consciousness at play with what it is to be in a body here and now. That's all. Ideally, as we play, we don't intentionally harm anyone. However, there will be times when we cause pain without meaning to. We will be an impetus to both joy and pain in this life. We can work to minimize the pain that we cause. Yet, that we will feel and cause harm is inescapable.

Ask yourself —"How do I choose to show up today no matter what anyone else might think about it/me?"

FACTS:

Liminal spaces—the "in-between"—are often seen as uncomfortable, yet they hold transformative power. A study published in the Journal of Applied Psychology (2020) found that individuals trained to embrace ambiguity showed a 35% improvement in problem-solving abilities and adaptability. Similarly, organizations that adopted non-binary frameworks in workplace policies reported a 20% increase in employee satisfaction and retention, according to Forbes Insights (2022).

Turning Times

R EFLECT:

- *What can you do to create the world you want to live in?*
- *How would you choose to show up no matter what happens or doesn't?*
- *In what ways can you re-imagine connecting with people new to you?*

When young, queer, and marginalized people have no support or role models for the non-standard ways that they feel they are or for the life that they want to live, they often feel shame for being different. They have to do tremendous inner work to survive and thrive. That work is mirrored now by the work that needs to be done by all of us for all beings to survive and thrive on our shared planet. It is time we all learned how to self-investigate and love a little bigger.

We are in a time of a great turning, a time of revealing. Nothing will be hidden in this time. It is as the tower in the tarot, a time of crumbling archaic structures, the falling away of the known. Harmful, repressive, divisive constructs of mind are dissolving, and we can no longer ignore them. That which steals from life shrivels in the light of unconditional loving awareness-presence. Neither truth nor toxicity can be ignored in this time if we want to survive on this planet. This mess we're in is moving us towards healing. Yet, transition times can be disarming and confronting. In this era, many of us find ourselves in fractured relationships with our selves, our work, and our families. We may be re-evaluating what really matters to us in this world.

In the space of the void left by what was no longer working, it is going to take the courage and brilliance of cultural revolutionaries, creative seers and thinkers, artists and dreamers to vision, share, and bring the new world into being. It begins within ourselves and our ability to live in mystery, to become comfortable in the uncertainty. It begins within our families and communities—how do we truly create more inclusive and harmonious environments? It is being with the unknown that leads us to the known.

"We want and deserve spaces that delight and marvel in the pleasures of difference. Rather than simply accepting that people are different, there is so much possibility and so much richness that comes from the fact that we're all different. Trying to eliminate that and constrict it into templates or binaries is not a good idea, not only for queer and trans people, it impoverishes everyone."

—Avgi Saketopoulou, Psychoanalyst, NYU Scholar, & co-author, along with Ann Pelligrini of the book *Gender Without Identity. Quote from KPFA program, Against the Grain interview w/ the authors, July 2024*

{ **32** }

Imagine If...

Write an essay or scene based on the prompts below. Do it with others and share notes, images, world-building exercises, and games to help dream us into a more loving, inclusive, and just future for all.

Imagine if *we didn't tell any child how they should look or dress before they had a chance to approach life with natural curiosity and wonderment.*

What if we didn't tell anyone how they should act, laugh, cry, or love based on their genitals?

Imagine having all of the space needed to learn and grow from our own so-called "mistakes" without seeing ourselves as failures.

What if we were told that our choices or behaviors could be beneficial or harmful without being told that we were good or bad based on our choices?

Imagine being taught the safe and practical use of things while simultaneously being invited to wonder how things work, what's possible, and what your part might be in creating reality.

This, below, is my expanded "imagine if" based on the prompts above. We need more expansive visions of what is possible in this life. All things begin in the imagination. Here is a peek into mine:

First, imagine that all humans spend more time communing with nature, feeling the wonder and awe of the fantastic variations of form, color, gender, and relational expressions that life takes! I imagine we would all be more in love with ourselves and each other if we lived with more awe and wonder.

Imagine if when a womb-bearer was pregnant, no one asked, "What are you having?" because we all knew that they were most likely having a baby! Perhaps we all wish them blessings on their pregnancy, wishes for a smooth birth, and wishes for a healthy child.

At the baby shower, we offer a rainbow of blessings—all the practical things needed in all the colors or perhaps whatever the parents feel for their baby. We know some babies come in with colors and names, conception stories, and dreams delivered to their kin that might guide these things. We understand that some of these things reveal themselves with birth and growth.

We, as a family and community, watch the baby grow and follow their own inclinations as to what interests them and what they might like to try. Do they sing, dance, want to be in the kitchen, climb trees, or play in the garden? Are they nurturing? A storyteller? Do they like to build things? Are they very physical and protective? Are they especially drawn to animals or any particular kind of people or work? As the child grows, we allow their natural proclivities to develop. We give them outfits and implements that match their natural interests. Sports teams are, like wrestling or boxing, rated by size/weight and not gender so that anyone can play any sport that they want to. All of our children are loved and supported by the whole community. We see that they naturally want to learn things and be an active part of their family and community. Each being easily fulfills the roles needed for their own actualization as well as for the thriving of their environment.

Elders who live in honored roles gently guide each being in learning their way in family and culture. They are celebrated for their wisdom, truth, and integrity. Self-love and respect for life are naturally occurring phenomena in all beings, and their natural being is encouraged and supported. All beings are witnessed and celebrated for their mental, intellectual, emotional, and physical growth and achievements.

Imagine a world where we give each other space to try on new talents, skills, modes of dress, styles of self-expression, ways of communicating, connecting, and loving. There is no "wrong" or "bad" choice on one's personal path unless it is with intent to harm oneself or others.

Imagine if, on any given day, you could wake up and wear whatever you wanted without being judged or challenged. Imagine loving someone just because of their kindness or how they inspire you to be a better person, no matter their gender, religion, or skin color. Imagine there are restrooms, clean water, nourishment, and welcoming spaces for all beings everywhere.

If it were the case that someone acted out maliciously or intentionally hurt themselves or another being, we would call a healing circle. Anyone could call a healing circle for themselves at any time. These circles are akin to restorative justice circles, sourced from the ways that many Indigenous peoples from North America, Africa, and Australia have historically dealt with conflict, crime, and injustice.

We would all want to understand why the offender(s) would harm themselves or another—what do they need? Are they hurting? What can help reconnect them to earth, self, community, and spirit? All of the community would care for and support their healing as we know it is for the greatest good for all.

Yes, I am a dreamer and a believer in the innate goodness of souls that inhabit bodies. There may be exceptions, as absolutes are never true, but we, as collectives, can search for ways to care for all beings. As I wrote this, some of it seemed so trite and obvious, but sadly, most of this is not the current norm. Some of this book may give rise to defensive responses. I would like to engage in dialogues with those who disagree, and I believe that it would serve the healing of our cultures for all of us to do so. This is far from a total picture but just laid out as a place to begin to dream and dialogue. How would you add to or change this vision? Why? What else might have given you permission, relief, support, or inspiration on your path? What else is possible?

Reflection: Where Do I Stand?

W rite &/or discuss;

- *What do I truly want from life, connection, and community?*
- *Where do I stand at this time regarding potent current issues? Why?*
- *What calls to be expressed through me?*
- *What parts of myself have I left behind, or tried to, that have been holding me back or causing me distress?*
- *How can I help create more harmonious inner and outer environments?*
- *How can I become more comfortable with not knowing?*

"What we call the beginning, is often the end, and to make an end is to make a beginning, the end is where we start from."
—TS Elliot

{ 34 }

Spells & Rituals

The spells and rituals in the following chapter are designed to help you integrate the learning and inspirations you have encountered in this book.

We can consume lots of media and get inspired all day long, but if we do not actively engage with the content and our subconscious mind, then there will be little to no lasting effects. If you want to make changes in your automatic habits and belief systems, then it takes repetition, symbolism, and some level of intensity to make the changes stick. When we push our edges or when we are pushed out of our comfort zone, that's when we experience lasting brain changes. Rituals and spells serve this purpose and can be repeated for the fullest effect.

Use this book as a reference, and come back to it often. Do the exercises with friends and community. There is a chapter at the end of the book and PDFs of the exercises online that will help you to do this work with others. We grow more in a community when we are witnessed and share our experiences. Most of our wounds were acquired in relationship and require being in relationship with others to heal. Healing communities can be found in spiritual or religious settings, through classes and workshops, activism and organizing, in both giving and receiving social services, self-help groups, and more.

As you become familiar with the rituals and exercises, you will likely find that they become yours, with your own creativity and inspiration arising to guide you.

FACTS:

Rituals can be powerful tools for healing. Research from Stanford University (2018) shows that people who engage in structured rituals, such as journaling or visualization, experience a 25% decrease in stress and an increase in emotional clarity. Similarly, expressive arts therapy, which often incorporates ritual elements, has been shown to improve resilience by up to 40%, according to the American Art Therapy Association (AATA).

{ 35 }

Ancestor Spell

Let's take a moment to honor all of the lives that have been lost to the crisis of binary thinking and the violence that it perpetuates in this world.

Remember that we stand upon the shoulders of courageous activist ancestors and transcestors who stood up against bigotry, sometimes at the cost of their lives.

We exist in a world formed and informed by these people's lives and work. We are blessed with freedoms and permissions won through the fights and sacrifices of our activist ancestors. It is our response-ability to remember the gifts we have been given and the privileges we have due to those who came before us on this revolutionary path of healing divides and awakening to our interconnectedness.

We now have the power and ability to advance their work and carve the way for those who will come after us. Those of us doing this work are part of a lineage of powerful spiritual leaders, activists, artists, witches, cultural rebels, and healers who have lit the way and passed the torch on.

Please speak the names of your activist ancestors. Name aloud those we have loved and lost in the struggle to expand unconditional love, safety, and acceptance for all.

"The dead have a pact with the living."
—Sweet Honey in the Rock, Breaths

Beloved Ancestors,
Thank you for all of the ways that you worked to bring truth,
justice, and love to this world
May your work and your lives be remembered and honored.
May your work and love live on through us.
May our love and attention be part of the solution
that enables all variations of colorful, courageous
beings to thrive.
May all beings of all identities, colors, shapes, and abilities
have all that they need to thrive.
Please support us as you can on this journey of healing and
reclaiming.
May love prevail.
May you rest in power.

Let us now take a few silent breaths of reflection to honor the
activist ancestors, known and unknown, whose shoulders we stand
upon and for all those who may have perished feeling unloved and
unaccepted. We remember you, we honor you. Thank you. May we
do our part to expand love and freedom in this world.

Looking back, we can recognize all that has changed and
our power to make change.

We have all been blessed and cursed with the wisdom *and* baggage of our ancestors. We are not separate in our individuality, after all; we are all a continuum of lineages. As we awaken to it, we can uplift or rectify what has come to us. This ritual reflection aims to help heal inherited trauma. Seeing our current situation clearly is often the beginning of dispelling the toxicity of the past.

I want to acknowledge how often ancestors are spoken of with such reverence and how often they did things that hurt and harmed people and nature. We do not need to revere them entirely, but we can learn from them. Was this done out of their ignorance, the ignorance of the time, or the fact that they suffered from abuse and oppression?

No matter what, whether we are honoring the receiving of their wisdom or gaining knowledge by reflecting on their follies, it is worth looking at the past as we have been told so that we do not repeat the same mistakes and can grow into better futures.

To begin, build yourself an altar or art piece that holds images and memories of your ancestors and/or the time/place in which they lived. Take some time to reflect on and write answers to the questions below. As you find your answers, you might find yourself with the resolve to cherish, celebrate, and motivate in new ways. See what arises and make an intention to live your best life for those who came before you who could not live as you can now and for those for whom you will be an ancestor.

With the prompts below, light a candle as you commune with your ancestors, tune into the times that they lived in, and reflect on your inheritance.

- What freedoms do we have that our ancestors did not?
- What do these freedoms enable us to do or respond to in this lifetime?
- What response-ability do we have to those who have gone before us and fought for these freedoms and abilities?
- What is available to us that was not available to those who have gone before?
- What does this enable us to do that our ancestors couldn't have imagined?
- What have we learned from the suffering of our ancestors? From their struggles?
- What can we learn from their mistakes?
- What were your ancestors' rituals? How did your ancestors honor the earth?
- What spirituality have you learned from your ancestors that serves life?
- What chains are you breaking in this lifetime? What changes would you make to what has been handed down to you?
- What limiting constructs of mind are you ready and able to dispel? How? Why? With what knowledge, freedom, or time?

- What responsibilities do we have that our ancestors did not or were ignorant of?
- Considering all of these things, what is your role to play in the world?

To help maintain the awareness and inspiration realized through these reflections, I suggest that you keep an ancestor altar and light a candle daily or regularly, light some incense, or anoint yourself with something that feels good to you as you honor your lineage and the work that you are doing. Regularly, take moments to honor and remember your ancestors' long journey and the wisdom you have cultivated from your reflections.

Put this altar and your writing together, somewhere unique and accessible so that when you feel despair, you can remind yourself of your blessings and inspirations.

When you feel ready, take some time to write out your personal story based on the prompts that you thought through while creating your ancestor altar. This essay will be a powerful reminder. Return to it. Re-read it and re-write it. I have included my own version below to serve as inspiration if needed.

My Ancestor Inspiration Story

I am no one's property. No one owns me or tells me what to do. I can live where I want to, travel to most places, date and love whomever I want, and do the work I am inclined to do. I can meet my basic needs, dress how I want, and write and say what I want. I have the freedom to vote. These things were not the truths of my female or queer ancestors.

I have a voice and can create and find many platforms to amplify my voice.

I have leagues of women and their allies to celebrate and give thanks to for many of these freedoms. Many women were beaten and jailed for their resistance to being the property of their husbands or fathers and did not have individual citizenship/human rights. Thank you to all those who have fought (and still do!) for the rights and freedom of women and oppressed beings worldwide. The fights and wins around these causes have given permission and inspiration to others to stand up for their freedoms. I am grateful, motivated, and supported by those who have come before me. The response-ability I have is to continue this work and to help ensure there is no going backward. May we continue to evolve and forge forward into the expansion of rights, freedom, and care for all beings.

I am grateful for the web of connection via technology in my lifetime. I can find people like myself who are struggling with, celebrating, or working on the same things as me and share resources and information. Where once we may have been isolated within a strict family or religion, now I have access to the world's wisdom. I have healing and inspiration literally at my fingertips. With that, I have spaces to ask questions, express myself, and formulate my ideas.

Some of my ancestors were indigenous peoples of this continent that we call North America, both the US & Canada, who fought and hid to survive persecution and genocide. They were Mi'kmaq, Iriquois, Blackfoot, and possibly Cherokee. I didn't know anything about them until I was in my 20s. It was a family secret.

My ancestors were shamed, scourged, silenced. They watched their lands and people being decimated. My ancestors were afraid to be who they were, to admit their heritage. They escaped to new places and tried to erase their pasts.

My maternal grandfather's mother had been the medicine woman of her tribe. She was of the Mi'kmaq tribe in Canada and, later, New England. They also had Blackfoot, Iroquois, and French in their family line. They immigrated to the US from Quebec but claimed only their French ancestry because of the danger and racism here. It wasn't any better there; they still experienced racist violence. My great-grandmother used to sneak out into the woods in her ceremonial garb with my grandfather and teach him about the healing plants. He was forced to go to an "Indian" reform school. There, he said he had his "language beaten out of" him by the nuns. He was told not to sing in the choir but to fake it because of his accent. He never told us these things until he was dying of Parkinson's and other health complications in his 80s. Even then, my grandmother would shush him and say, "Pete, we don't talk about those things!".

We do not have to hide these things anymore.

My maternal grandmother's parents died young. She became the big sister-mother of her family of 12 and worked in the factories to help feed and care for the children. She always told us when we would try to get her to play, "I don't play games." (she said in a very firm, 'do not question me' voice). She was stern, often harsh, and practical but also took great joy in caring for others her whole life. She taught me by example how to stay 'no-nonsense' and active in joyful service to others through hard times.

I did not know my Irish/Scottish/Spanish/Blackfoot & possibly Cherokee paternal grandparents very well because my dad was abusive and drug/alcohol dependent. My mother left him when I was 4 years old. He found us again when I was 19. His mom was still alive for a while, so I got to know her a bit. He was the youngest in a very proud Irish-identified family. His alcoholic dad regularly beat him. When his father's family came to the US from Ireland, escaping famine and war, they were shamed and seen as low-caste. They lived in Oklahoma and had a farm with ten kids who, the story goes, were taken outside and lined up on Saturday mornings for their beatings just so that none of them would "get out of line" and so that they were afraid to. In these lands, the Blackfeet and possibly Cherokee tribes also became my ancestors. Again, these were considered shameful mixings at the time, and no one talked about or honored the heritage and traditions.

My mother is not yet an ancestor, but many of her ways of being were formed by the trauma of her ancestors. She suffered violent sexual trauma when she was still a kid with hopes and dreams that then became shattered. Her mother shamed and cursed her for what happened to her. She had no offering of healing for her trauma. She cursed and shamed me in similar ways simply for being female and vivacious. I was taught to shut up, keep my legs closed, and be ashamed of my body, sexuality, voice, and self-expression. As a kid, I thought she was cruel in making me stay small. I see now that it was a way that she tried to protect me.

My biological father also perpetuated the abuse and trauma handed down to him. He has spent many years now apologizing for it. I acknowledge that the abuse and silencing that were imposed upon me as a child were handed down from the traumas of the generations before me and my parents. I recognize now, as a long-term healing adult, that they all did the best they could with the resources they had.

We are all still growing and healing. Humans live to grow, heal, learn, love, and dream.

I am grateful to be resourced. I am thankful to have a voice. I am blessed to have support systems and permissions from my spirit family, community, and the world. As messed up as this country is, I am also lucky to live here in the US and have the privileges that we do. I am made for this time—a big, loud-mouthed, empathic, body-positive, dancing, rebel-fire child, ready to face the messy world and help tear down the crumbling, expired constructs and systems that have held down and hurt so many.

I honor the wisdom of those who have come before and gain insight by reflecting on their follies. I take courage and response-ability from this looking and seeing.

I break chains of silence and shame. I speak my truth, courageously reveal all that my ancestors and I have been ashamed of, and dispel the shame with honor.

I sing for my ancestors who could not sing their songs!

I am here to help heal the traumas we have been taught to be ashamed of and hide from. I have the courage and permission to protect myself and speak the truth to and about those who have harmed me. I invite those who have been harmed into healing and honor their pain and what they have had to do to be okay.

I am blessed with the tools and resources for healing that are now more widely available than ever.

I reclaim full ownership and honor my vibrant, multi-faceted sexuality and pleasure body! I do it for my mothers. May you live joyously, silly, playful, and ecstatic through me. May I revel in the gifts of my senses.

Finally, a great response-ability that our recent ancestors might not have attended to is caring for the earth. As the world's spiritual traditions moved away from being earth-based, many cultures forgot their responsibility to the planet. She generously gives us everything we need. It is our job to return that love and take care of her.

Thank you to my grandfather who handed down the knowledge of gardening in cooperation with the earth, thank you to all of the earth guardians, land tenders, water protectors, tree protectors, farmers, activists, and environmentalists who work to keep our consciousness connected to humans' effect on the planet and what we must do to care for her if we want to keep eating and living off of her.

May I be counted among the ranks of earth guardians. May I do my best to protect and preserve our resources. May I stay connected and help others become aware of their integral connection to all of nature.

Remnants of my family's indigenous spirituality remain in my mother's knowledge of gardening and animal care. I will expand upon these.

From the work of reflecting and contemplating the above, the intention that has arisen for me, that I carry now resounding in my heart is;

I live in celebration of life on this earth; I am a voice for my ancestors.

36

Nona Fender's Angels & Demons

R itual Play
A playful practice for communing with and integrating estranged parts of ourselves

Who is Nona Fender?

When I moved to the SF Bay Area I became a circus performer, activist artist, and costume designer very involved with yoga, creative, and healing communities. I found my New York/New England self pleasantly welcomed into a softer, more light-hearted, sparkly world. I also found that my edgy East Coast sense of humor and my say-it-like-it-is bluntness and sarcasm were not well received by many of the more gentle beings I was encountering. Coming from my rough, *white trash* upbringing and NYC drag queen/fashionista culture, I found myself unintentionally offending people. There seemed to be no room in this glorious *love and light* for all the things that people are afraid to speak of–the 'shadow' aspects of humanity–guilt, shame, fear, sex, death, anger, rage, 'bad thoughts,' all the dirty, stinky, messy human stuff. I wanted the sweetness but also needed the ability and space to express the raw emotions of life, and I did not feel comfortable or understood when being more "rawr" in these new circles.

So, NONA FENDER was born as a persona to act out the things that did not feel socially acceptable in my new world. I was doing burlesque at the time and MC'ing fashion & burlesque shows. My dear fellow costumier and hairdresser friend, Ed Kittenhouse, began cattily calling me Nona Fender. I lept at the opportunity, "is this not someone's name already?" I asked cautiously, not wanting to get in a tangle with anyone who would take on the moniker of known offender. As far as the catty Kittenhouse knew, it wasn't. I began to MC as Nona, and then, since I had been practicing and teaching yoga for years, yoga started creeping into my audience interactions. People began to ask where they could take a class with Nona. So, I had to oblige. Nona Fender got together with her beloved musician partner EEnor & some other colorful friends and created a live music, movement, sound, and 'getting high breaths' set. I used theater games, vocal exercises, connection and self-expression practices, silly dance moves like air guitar and twerking, and weird things kids and ritualists do, and mixed them all together. I led class with a big trashy wig, too much makeup, lots of heavy gold jewelry, and a mosh-up of accents from my mom and my bestie in NYC. I acted like I didn't care and said offensive things while wearing tight, shiny clothes and stilettos (at least at the beginning of each set). The audaciously sexy, sacred-profane, comedic approach to it all actually ended up giving me permission to go even deeper into prayer and drama therapy than regular classes could do. It lured those who thought they would never do yoga. Nona's style led huge groups of party people to pray (to no specific God but just for the greatest good) together in the streets because we approached it through play. Studies have since shown that some of the most profound trauma healing happens through play.[17] Our first official gig as a band was a Fukushima Benefit, Spring 2011 @ Cloud 9, Berkeley. Before each event, I would sit with myself in the mirror and remind myself/this self, who I am (Nona Fender) and why I am doing this CRAZY thing that I am doing—dressing up in trashy clothes, too much makeup, and a terrible wig to lead YOGA!?!? Yup, trashy, too-sexy, messy, hesher-ratchet yoga-ish. Nona was FUNNY!, rude, impatient, snarky, demanding, messy, wrong, wrong, wrong...and THE MOST courageous, caring, loving, inspirational, permission-giving 'self' that I had ever been to that point. Those who could get past the 'wrong-ness' of what she/I was doing became inspired and were oh so grateful to be given *permission* (this is the word I heard over and over from participants) to be big, loud, honest, playful, free, fully expressed humans with NOTHING to be ashamed of! *That* was my *why*: to dispel shame and invoke highly charged, therefore effective, healing play. We grieved, we loved, laughed, we prayed, we played. We offended some serious yogis, and we kept on going to new frontiers.

I led experiences as Nona from 2010 to 2020, when the world changed, and so did I. The Nona parts of me have now integrated into my being, and she has only had a couple of guest appearances since the global COVID pandemic. But, despite being a little quieter these days, I continue to lead profound cathartic experiences in a spirit of play at the right times and places.

This is one of my favorite Nona Fender rituals. It was particularly effective and has lots of room for creativity in it. I had one of my Tantrik teachers witness this experience and say that it is actually a Tantrik practice to do what we were doing and act out one's demons in this way, embracing and exaggerating the fullness of their "I dare not," hidden, squashed, afraid aspects of self.

ANGELS & DEMONS

This is extra fun with a circle of friends, especially those who are actively embodied, playful, and have some performance experience. But really, anyone can do this—we did it as children in so many ways. This play can also be done alone, with a camera or at least a mirror so that you can PLAY WITH YOURSELF! Either way, we are looking for reflections of ourselves—in one another, on the screen, or in the mirror.

1. Create a container—a circle of beings or a circle for your selves to play in—real or imaginary. Welcome the fullness of everyone. Make this a safer place where all are welcome, all aspects of being, all beings. It can help to do some warm-up breath and movement practices first—the sillier, the more playful, the better.

2. Reflect for a moment on a part of you that makes you feel ashamed or afraid. Find something you were taught at some point is not okay or socially acceptable. What have you been taught in one way or another is 'too much' about you? What do you try to cover up with being 'nice,' quiet, or people-pleasing?

3. Imagine this aspect or way of being as a character all on its own. You can give them a name and story, see their offensiveness through their movement, posture, voice, and act it out. EXAGGERATE IT! Find a line or two to play with and a scenario to imagine as you do. Make it the full-blown cartoon version, the full-on villain character in the movie version! Have fun with it! Notice if it feels creepy or uncomfortable, and turn UP the volume on that!

If in a group, we use the group to mirror and exaggerate what comes through each of us. We all play with this aspect of ourselves together, interacting with one another in this exaggerated way of being. Blow it up until it just feels utterly laughable and ridiculous. Do laugh.

If you are recording yourself, go again after you watch the first one and see if you can maximize the effect you got the first time. Again, go for the ridiculous, over-the-top cartoon version of this way of being! Go until you see that this unexaggerated part of yourself is a friendly, normal, and entirely acceptable version of this human trait.

4. Shake it off. Shake your body. Touch the ground. Release. Ground. Reset. Find your center.

5. Now, imagine a way that you WISH you could show up more. See yourself in one of your most open, joyful, confident, winning, turned-on, fully expressed moments. What is a way that you WANT to be that you have been told or felt like was *too much*?

6. Play as this fullness again—go cartoon with it! Create a character, someone unabashed and freely expressed in all of their fantastic potential. Yes, this, too, is you. Have fun with it! How big can you go? How would this being interact with others? What is the dramatic edge of this one? What reality is revealed in this play about how you can give yourself more freedom to play in your day-to-day life? Play with and exaggerate these qualities until a slightly less exaggerated version feels like a normal way to be.

7. Shake it Off! Reflect on how it felt to go deep into these edges of being and where that might give you more freedom to show up with a little more fullness in everyday life. Do some writing or process with loved ones. Give this character a nickname in order to easily invoke and return to this part of you. Utilize an accessory or key costume piece that holds the energy of the permission to play you have just given yourself. Have it with you when you want to call this character up from the inside to support how you want to show up in particular moments in life.

For example, in this ritual, I have played with exaggerating bad leadership—being the bossy, bitchy self I am afraid of, and then encouraging participants to exaggerate it until it is just ridiculous. It now becomes like a cartoon self that I will recognize if I find myself acting that way, and I can laugh at that and remember the choices I have. It even got so those closest to me would say, "Okay, Nona," when I got a little too edgy in "real" life, and that would often dispel the tension with laughter.

On the flip side, I played with what it is to be unashamed of being big, bright, outspoken, having "look-at-me" moments, and standing in the spotlight with grace and pride. These things were natural to me as a young child but became difficult as a result of being shut down by my parents. Playing with that was fun and opened me up to remember the natural ways that kids are, that I was, and still get to be—without rebelliousness, shame, or self-judgment.

Seeing our problems and behaviors acted out and exaggerated outside of ourselves often dispels them, releases their power over us, and gives us objectivity and room for more options. The more we can be transparent and accept, embrace, share, make fun of ourselves, and play with the tendencies that arise, the more freedom we will have to CHOOSE how we want to show up.

PLEASE BE AWARE—This work can be triggering and intense. If you intend to use these deeper psychological exercises in groups, be familiar with the people you play with. Check in first. Know their mental states, whether or not they have training in yoga, acting, nervous system care, and other modalities that might be helpful. Start with a general check in, movement, grounding, breath, and connection games, and then move into bigger exercises like this. Leaders should be trained in facilitating theater games, counseling, &/or be trauma-informed. If possible, have an assistant who can support people who meet emotional challenges. Be VERY clear about what you are inviting people into! Try these things yourself and with smaller, more familiar groups and trusted individuals first.

37

The Badass Spell

It's fun to say Badass. But what do we mean? For me, a badass is a self-possessed person who is confident, calm, cool, and collected and doesn't freak out under pressure. A badass is a sovereign being who knows they need others and dares to ask for what they need without being needy. They can hold themselves and others through trying times. A badass speaks their truth and knows who they are despite what anyone else thinks or might have to say about them.

My friend A is a badass. At our *Dispelling the Binary* workshop at the Soul Play festival, A spoke about an upcoming family reunion and the fear and frustration surrounding their family's not understanding or respecting their gender and pronouns. They asked for support from the group and inquired what we should do in this situation. I invited them to imagine and share how they would idealize showing up in this situation. They said, "As a Badass."

What happened next was a beautiful, spontaneous spell, which I've written out for you here so that you can use it whenever you need some "Badass" energy or want to support another in remembering their powerful nature. Have the person you are attending choose their own verbiage and definition, "badass" or otherwise. Whatever words they use should resonate with and ideally come from the receiver.

OUTLINE for Honoring the Badass

- Have the receiving individual stand in the center of the space you're in.
- Invite them to speak aloud about the qualities and characteristics that they are calling in. Have the Badass imagine themselves fully feeling like the Badass version of themselves that they are. Instruct them to feel these qualities alive in their body, posture, and breath. Guide them to be open to any colors, shapes, or movements that arise that might be supportive of fully expressing their "badass" nature. Invite everyone to see this person *as* the Badass that they are.
- Invite the Badass to name anything they want to say, have heard, or known, and repeat their truth, "I am a Badass."
- Have the crowd repeat these affirmative statements, mirror back, and even amplify their power. i.e.; "You are a Badass!" or "A is a badass!"
- Invite the Badass to really feel this love, reflection, and affirmation from the audience (which could even be one person or a small group of friends). Have them really look around and take it in. A mirror can also be helpful here if you want to try this alone.
- Now, Badass, imagine yourself in the anticipated, challenging situation as you stay connected to the energy present in this moment. Feel your power, the web of connection of a community of spirit and beloveds who re-

late to you, know you, and/or support you. Create an imaginary bridge from the support and power of now into the situation before you.

- Sense the roots of the trees and mycelia beneath you, creating a big web from this space and moment into the one you will be in with your family. Feel the support of the earth as part of this community of spirit.
- Hold a mudra, a shape with the hand(s), or a way of holding your body, and breathe the strength and power of now into that form as a key to bring it with you into the future situation. Our bodies remember. Echoing these shapes and mantras in the future can bring us back to the memory of being supported in feeling our power even when we are in less supportive environments.
- End with a tremendous celebratory "I AM a Badass!" and everyone repeating it (or saying "You are a badass!") and cheering!

Repeat the mantra and mudra often to keep that energy alive within you. Take it anywhere you might feel challenged and want to remember this!

For the Solo Badass!—a hone alone version;

- Stand in front of a mirror.
- Speak aloud about the qualities and characteristics that you're calling in. Imagine yourself fully feeling like the Badass version of yourself that you are. Feel these qual-

ities alive in your body, posture, and breath. Be open to any colors, shapes, or movements that arise that might be supportive of fully expressing your "badass" nature. Imagine the world seeing you as a badass.

- Repeat your truth, "I am a badass."
- Hear these affirmative statements repeated back from the badass in the reflection.
- Feel this love and affirmation from your reflection. Really look, and take it in.
- Now, Badass, imagine yourself in the anticipated, challenging situation as you stay connected to the energy present in this moment. Feel your power, the web of connection of a community of spirit and beloveds who relate to you, know you, and support you. Create an imaginary bridge from the support and power of now into the situation before you.
- Sense the roots of the trees and mycelia beneath you, creating a big web from this space and moment into the one ahead of you that might be challenging. Feel the support of the earth as part of this community of spirit.
- Hold a mudra, a shape with the hand(s), or a way of holding your body, and breathe the strength and power of now into that form as a key to bring it with you into the future situation. Our bodies remember. Echoing these shapes and mantras in the future can bring us back to the memory of being supported in feeling our power even when we are in less supportive environments.
- End with a tremendous, celebratory "I AM a Badass!"

Repeat the mantra and mudra often to keep that energy alive within you. Take it anywhere you might feel challenged and want to remember this!

38

Alchemical Marriage Ritual

Integrate your learning, embrace all aspects of yourself, invoke a connection with all parts, inner & outer...

The idea of the Alchemical Marriage comes from traditions of alchemy, which arose in the Middle Ages, about 3500 BC. Jabir ibn Hayyan, an Islamic scholar, is known as the father of alchemy and chemistry as we know it. The roots of the art of alchemy are in Egypt and Arabia. It moved on to Greece and Rome and then to Western and Central Europe, where it became, and still is a lasting part of the Hermetic traditions of Magick.

The work of alchemy is about transmutation and transformation. The Alchemical Marriage is about bringing apparent opposites or disparate parts together to create a new version or to bring something fractured back to wholeness. Alchemical ideas have been integrated into both magickal and therapeutic systems (Internal Family Systems is an excellent example of how to do this work as a therapeutic process).

A visual representation for this ritual is 'The Lovers' tarot card, which is designed to represent the alchemical marriage.

This card, as well as the ritual, is not necessarily about uniting two individuals but first about unifying and harmonizing the masculine/feminine, fire/water, earth/sky, and/or light/dark aspects of ourselves. This can also be used to bring parts of ourselves back into the fold that we may have rejected, denied, ignored, or hidden away in reaction to trauma or a feeling of necessity due to circumstances in our environment. The alchemical marriage can be used to consciously marry oneself to the divine, using the process to remember and honor one's divine nature and inextricable relationship to "God/dess"/Dei'i. Finally, it can be used to celebrate the union of beloveds' divine selves to one other.

For our purposes here, we will focus on bringing the Self back to wholeness; through this practice, the Self and all its parts become unified. This ritual/ceremony could be done in many different ways. I offer an outline below, but I encourage you to weave in your own creativity, devotional objects/practices, and words. It is important that this kind of intimate ritual feels like yours. You can play with it until it does.

Rituals work by connecting to the subconscious mind, which also lives in the body. The subconscious mind works through symbols; it does not so quickly receive messages and adapt to change through words alone. We are able to pattern the subconscious through symbolism, repetition, and high-impact or 'peak' experiences. We raise energy through embodied song, rhythm, dance, chanting/vocalizing, acting out/repetition of symbolic action like union (this can include love-making—to self or other), evocative movement, and relative, heightened states of conscious awareness.

Prepare yourself some nourishing, grounding food, and have some water on hand for the end of the ritual. These could be on the altar and ingested towards the end of the ritual as part of it. Or you can feast to celebrate and ground once the ritual union is enacted. Feeding the beloved self and/or the perceived other is an act of love and devotion.

The ritual begins in the planning. Watch out as you may hear or meet serendipitous, supporting situations and beings along the way. Keep your attention open for objects and inspirations that resonate with your intention. Use these for the creation of the altar*, or a centerpiece that holds the energy of the intention for your focus. This can also be represented by works of art that you make for the purpose. You do not need to go out and buy any fancy implements unless you want to. (Especially if it supports your local artists or magick stores, then go for it!). Nature provides.

Intention—reflect on your intention. What are you looking to harmonize or unite with this ritual? Be as clear and succinct as you can and create a 1-3 line intention that is easy to repeat and holds the power and energy of your intended outcome. Be sure that it is present tense and affirmative to really hold the energy of what you *desire* becoming *manifest in the here-now*. It is fun and potentially 'stickier' if it is poetic, evocative, and easy to repeat/chant/sing. But it could be very simple, as in,

"I AM THAT". i.e.; "I am in harmony with all parts of my-self. We celebrate our fullness as One". Rather than, 'I want to be in fullness', etc.. focus on the realization and let it dispel any feeling of lack. What we focus on grows, so focus on what you want to grow and how that will feel when realized, not on what you feel is wrong or missing. This is a foundational principle of magick and mental wellness.

*The ALTAR—bring together items or images that represent your intention, your Self, your whole Self, and the Part(s) of yourself that you are working with. This could be photos, keepsakes, jewelry, murtis, toys, etc. Or create an image with whatever your preferred artistic medium is today. Gather and include things that hold the energies you are calling in. Have a center point, ideally, an image or representation that exudes wholeness and joy, something that represents the realized "you" that your ritual is for.

If you are working with bringing wounded parts of yourself back into the fold of your loving awareness, gather things that represent those parts of self that have been exiled or ignored. These things will frame the centerpiece.

If you are working on marrying (i.e.;the masculine and feminine) parts of Self, then they can both hold center together since that is the goal.

If the ritual is to connect to the divine in another being, then you both will add things that have meaning for and represent you in all of your fullness.

Bring in items that represent the natural elements or tools to interact with the elements, i.e.; a bowl of water, earthy things, incense/scents, candles or light, etc. Get as many senses involved in your ritual as you can.

Add any sacred objects representing your Divine cohorts: God/dess, Dei'i, spirit, angels, guides, fae, etc., any of the invisible forces that you might call upon to support your ritual and healing.

Ritual Body

Cast the circle—once you have created your centerpiece, then cast/draw a circle with salt, ash, water, a wand, your finger, or your imagination. Any of these things will do. This is for the purpose of creating a safe place of focus and a container for your magick. Silence all distractions as possible. Focus your mind and energy into this space. Ask for permission and support from the land and the spirits of the land that you are on.

Ground—Feel your connection to earth, breath, and the moment. Practice any movements, sounds, or self-care that help you (and other participants if you are not alone) ground and fully land in the moment, in the body.

Intention—repeat your intention three times

Invocations*—call in the elements of nature, spirit guides, ancestors, divine supports, inspirations, anything/one that supports life as you know and want it. Speak to, and if you would like, leave offerings and representations of these elements/energies around the cardinal points (N, E, S, W) of your circle, the directions/ elements vary with traditions, but the ones I have experienced most commonly are; N - Earth, E - Air, South - Fire, West - Water. Then add the in-between, or queer, directions if you'd like, i.e.; mud, steam, dust, sparks, etc. at NW, SW, NE, & SE respectively. Usually the Center is recognized as a place of Spirit/Divine, and Above and Below are also acknowledged as places of other, unseen elements, beings, and supports.

Invite the elemental energies and with that all that we are composed of, to harmonize with your intention, i.e.; water is cleansing, moves things, etc. This could help to wash away old ideas and limiting beliefs, you can act this out (or take a ritual bathing!) Water is the energy of fluidity, helping us to soften rigidity and welcome the fluid nature of our being into its natural state. What do each of the elements represent for you and how might your attention to them serve your intention? You can look to ancient traditions for the meaning and resonance of these elements or just use your intuition and imagination.

Interact with each in turn in a way that feels like a celebration and supports your intention. As much as you can, make these *embodied* actions. Engage all of the senses possible. Move your body, make some noise, light candles, use oils or incense, and engage with the elements.

Divine Energies—Include prayer, song, chant or offerings to whatever spiritual/divine energies you are calling in. Ask for what you want. Give thanks for what you have.

Bless All Parts of the Self (& perhaps, each other), touch and speak to all parts of yourself (&/or your beloved). You can anoint each part with sacred oils, gentle kisses, or touch each part with an athame or other sacred instrument. Thank each part for how it has served you in your life, for its presence and any blessings, and acknowledge any key challenges connected to any parts which have inspired learning and growth. Give thanks and appreciation as fully as you can to all parts.

Let Go!—Speak to what needs to be transmuted, to what you are giving up, feel what needs to be felt—this may be a time to scream, shake, cry, rage, surrender, or carry out a ritual act of release—bury it, burn it, throw it up into the air...give it to the elements and divine to be transmuted. When done this part, repeat your intention, that which you wish the energy of the thing we are letting go of to be transmuted into.

Raise Energy—Return to what you are calling in. Speak your vows or intentions, pray, give what you know, and invite what you don't know of yourself to this dedication. Continue to raise energy to a peak, and direct it towards your intention. Move your body, play a drum, play your body, find a rhythm, sway, dance, bounce, shake, chant, and/or do breath practice. Build physical intensity and arousal. You can make your own music or put on an instrumental or inspirational track that lifts you up. You could also create an improvised piece of art here as your energy-raising practice. You can even clean or rearrange your environment as representative of your subconscious mind or life. Get creative. Whatever you do should resonate with your spirit as well as perhaps expand your edges beyond your comfort zone. That is where magick lives, after all.

Gather—Pause to gather up the energy that you are cultivating. Open your arms wide and literally move as though you were gathering up something and bring it into your heart or wherever your bodymind needs healing. Do this multiple times. Direct the energy you raise to your intention.

Direct—Intensively imagine the life force energy that is present sinking in and becoming your healing, your strength, your vital, truthful expression of self out into the world. See/speak the energy into the intention. I am that. So it is. Act it out. Hold a powerful pose/shape in your body and shine it out. See/speak your truth into your environment, into the situations and relationships in your life. Here is where you might also speak your vows to self or other, rich with the energy you have just raised.

Ground—once you are done working with the big energy that you have raised, send it up and out into the world, and then ground. Touch your body, touch the earth. Send the energy back into the earth. Feel yourself held, grounded, and supported. Give back to that which has nourished you. Take a pause in relative stillness and silence. You might Om, tone, sigh, or humm to help the grounding. Ultimately, rest in receptivity to integrate and receive any messages from aspects of self or spirit guides. Hugging of self or other is also grounding.

Reflect: What steps can you take in your life to support this new way of being? Name at least the first three. What support from others can you call in? Is there someone that you might share your experience with who can help you keep your intention as a focus for your healing?

To complete this part of the ritual, it could be helpful to have some dialogue, writing, and/or meditation time. Answer the above questions and consider what else might keep the energy of this ritual intention expanding and blossoming into its fullness in your life.

Release—give thanks to all of the energies, elements, and spirits that you called in and for whatever you have received. Give thanks and appreciation to any other participants. Open the circle. This is all part of the ritual. Stay present and focused. The effects of ritual do not land all at once. A shift or realization could happen at any time. Further integration could show up through new happenings, connections, or dreams. Clean up and return any implements used to places of honor. Hang your art, and put ritual items away with care. Offer any natural altar offerings to the trees, waters, and land around you.

Eat some food and drink some water to help the grounding and digestion of your experience.

Keep a small altar up, or hang your art somewhere central to be seen by you for remembrance and integration in the days to follow. The ritual and digestion of the experience might continue in the days to come with dreams, serendipitous meetings, conversations, bits overheard or read, or seemingly randomly but poignant occurrences. Stay mindful and open to the possibilities.

Remember—the subconscious mind is a mysterious place that expresses itself through the body. All that we take in sensorily affects it. Give yourself some space after and around ritual away from news, social media, violent, or otherwise disturbing entertainment, or vacuous conversations. Keep your personal container—your body and time/space protected for a while as ritual effects could be gestating and arising for days or weeks. Keep your intention present daily for a moon cycle or longer if you can. Repeat it, embody it, do the movement of gathering up energy: emotion, elements, etc, and install it in your heart with the repetition of your intention. Magick and healing are often slow, mysterious, and beyond words happenings. Wait for it. Stay present and open. Commune with nature and beings that inspire you.

More resources for ritual magick can be found on my website.

{ 39 }

Final Reflections

A *peek back at the big picture.*
As many wise beings have said, when anyone suffers, we all suffer. Rigid identifiers can keep us feeling separate and enable violence toward the perceived other, including nature. Mindful attention to our connectedness is the medicine for the 'us vs them' binary which perpetuates the majority of our ails.

Living in a world with so many pressing environmental and social issues can feel overwhelming. We want to do *something*, but choosing *what* is most important and *how* to make a difference can feel impossible. Often, the same work must be done on all levels, from micro to macro, hence my invitation to peek at the big picture before we wrap up.

As per data up to late 2024, the World Health Organization estimates that each year we have over 720,000 deaths by suicide worldwide. Of course, that doesn't take into account accidental deaths by overdose or risk-taking behaviors caused by people hating themselves and each other. Humanity has been committing ecocide for generations, and now the sick systems we have created are killing *us*. We suffer from sick systems of "health," toxic food growth and production, oppressive legal and financial systems, and a lack of access to communal resources. This is because we see ourselves as separate from the earth and from one another, based on an ingrained "us vs them" or "man vs nature" binary mindset.

Neglect and destruction of our natural ecosystems by government, big business, and the exceedingly wealthy lower the quality of life for all of us. This separatist, othering behavior is causing toxicity in all of our ecosystems: earthly, social, and economic. Our primal fears are being poked at as we experience the devastating effects of the climate crisis, war, and extremism. Us-and-them binary thinking is heightened and often used as a weapon and false sense of security in these states of fear.

The work highlighted in this book is the work each of us can do in our inner microcosms to free ourselves individually. Ultimately, this is the same work that the macrocosm of our world communities needs to attend to. We must find unity in our diversity and honor the perceived "other" if we hope to find resourceful ways to support surviving and thriving on this earth for all beings. The healing invitation is to recognize the Self we are connected to in all beings.

As we do this work for ourselves and our intimate relationships, see that it's the same work we must do on the grand scale for planetary well-being. Look at the state of the world today and see that othering and ideas of separation are what we are bombarded by in politics and the media. Look at the bulk of the problems that we individually and collectively contend with, which are, at their root, based on fear of the other.

The 'us and them' binary leads to scarcity mindsets and violent reactivity. The solution, at its essence, is the same—to focus on our wholeness and interconnectedness. Whatever our skin color, gender, religion, or lifestyle, while alive on this planet, we are at one with the life of the planet. Beings who live close to the earth know this. As a species, we may have largely forgotten for a time, but we are remembering. This work is about remembering.

In this time, we are collectively dismantling many worn-out constructs. We are remembering more of the interconnected nature of reality and, with it, ourselves and those with whom we share this planet. We are moving towards healing generations of traumatic other-ing that continue to cause violence and pain.

Curiosity and compassion are the primary tools and medicines for this work. It can be messy, painful work, but it is essential to our growth and awakening to interconnectedness. Ultimately, it is a joyful, life-giving, life-serving work that we will feel good about when our time here is up.

Thank you for being on this journey with me. Maybe you are a workshop leader or teacher using this book as a resource for leading a workshop. Perhaps this is a solo journey that you have begun. I hope that these investigations will inform your life and offerings. Thank you for taking the time to read, reflect, and share what moves you with me or those around you in any way that might inspire healing or connection.

I wish you to feel inspired and empowered to express your-self more fully in ways you may not have felt permission to do before. If the ways that you want to dance and sing in this world do not intentionally hurt anyone, then please know that **you have permission to express yourself freely**. You are sup-ported by a growing community of healers, leaders, teachers, storytellers, historians, artists, creators, spiritual guides, cul-tural rebels, tricksters, and courageous hearts of all sorts who are questioning an expired consensus reality and finding new and evolved truths that center love, acceptance, freedom, in-clusion, and thriving for all people, animals, plants, and the whole of our planet.

A common denominator in most spiritual and philosophi-cal traditions is everything/one being seen as connected, inter-connected, love, God/dess, Dei'i, Divine, the universe at play, vibration discovering itself through the sense organs of these bodies. Within this worldview, everything experienced is un-derstood to be for learning and growth—all of it. To live life fully, to become awakened to realities beyond our social con-ditioning, and to die without regret, we will benefit from thor-oughly knowing and embracing ourselves. I encourage you to accept your perceived failures as intrinsic lessons here at Earth School.

All parts of ourselves will show up in some way at some point—often in distorted ways if we ignore them. The ignored and rejected aspects remain and will 'act out' if repressed. All aspects of self/life want expression. Some parts, when ignored, become sicknesses of the bodymind, and we end up hurting ourselves and others. So, the play I am inviting you into is life-saving. This is why I have found acting and play so helpful in integrating and digesting our fears and traumas. When we engage with the subconscious, we get closer to unity consciousness. When we investigate ourselves and our environments with curiosity and wonder, we expand our experience of *the love that we already are.*

We are always whole but will feel broken when we ignore or reject any part of ourselves. This feeling of brokenness can also arise when others reject parts of us. Still, ultimately, it is up to us to hold ourselves in compassionate curiosity and learn how to be our own parents, best friends, and beloveds. Yes, we will have many others who play these roles throughout our lives, but we are each the only embodied One we will have with us for this lifetime. All others will come and go. It is so important to remember this.

I invite you again and again to remember that no matter what you are *experiencing,* you are not that experience. You are the universe, dancing with all it is to be human. The universe is you. You are the stage that the universe is playing the role of you upon. Why? To experience what it is to be *this* embodiment in *this* lifetime. How does *this* set of sense-receptors perceive the world and respond to it? How is life inspired to express itself through *this* body right now? And, whatever your answer is NOW, it will continue to change. That's part of the fun.

Here are some suggestions to deepen your daily explorations:

- Have more meaningful conversations about things that move you.
- Read more inspiring books and talk about them with others.
- Experiment with new ways of dressing and expressing yourself. Keep investigating who you would be without preconceived identities.
- Go to new places and engage with people from different walks of life.
- Dedicate to integrating 1-3 of the practices or rituals in this book into your daily life for a couple of weeks each. Take notes on your experience.

When we resist, limit, or fully identify with only one aspect of being or some prescribed, "acceptable" set of traits, we resist our fullness. Limited identities limit our life force energy and effectiveness in this world. Beyond any old limiting stories or beliefs inherited from people who lived in an entirely different time and place—what feels true for you now? What makes sense for *this* body in *this* time and place?

There is much to honor and maintain that has been received from our ancestors of blood and spirit. But, let us not do it by rote, fear, or habit—let us live with truth, discernment, choice, curiosity, and wonder about what else is possible. What serves life here, now?

We have too long observed the damage done by humanity's ignorance, fear, and cruelty towards the unknown or the perceived "other." Now, we get to choose to perpetuate it or...

DISPEL THAT SHIT!

{ 40 }

Use This Book

Once you have done this work for yourself (on your own or in a small book-club-style group), I invite you to use this book to create a community connection workshop for your family, school, group, or organization in order to help folx understand each other and themselves better by connecting with authenticity and vulnerability on the things that we don't often talk about but obviously need to. A community connection workshop has the ability to bring deeper empathy, compassion, permission, and freedom into your communities. Help your teachers, leaders, parents, managers, bosses, guides, counselors, and so forth to know themselves and help understand those that they care for a little better. This is the work that makes the world a better place. To bridge worlds and make connections to the perceived other is the medicine that heals. Accepting and celebrating the multi-dimensional self and the unity in our diversity makes life rich and wonderful for all.

In order to begin creating your workshop, first be sure that you have done all of the exercises and integrated your learning. It is important to know the effect that these exercises have to feel familiar and resonate with what you are bringing. Then, go through the book again and highlight what feels most important to you to share with your school, family, and communities. Notice what feels edgy to you or makes you nervous. That might be the most important stuff. Then you can:

- Use the table of contents and/or your highlighted phrases as an outline for your workshop.
- Choose 3-5 exercises and the information necessary to set those up and support them for a complete workshop.
- Create a dedicated book club for practitioners! Have everyone read the book and then meet for group discussions and exercises.

There are PDFs of the lists and exercises on the Dispelling the Binary page online @www.lucidyoga.com, and an e-version of the whole book is also available wherever digital books are sold so that you can print the pages for your group. You may also find information about upcoming courses and retreats where we will work with these themes and practices together. Sign up for the newsletter @lucidyoga.com to keep updated.

The deeper rituals at the end are best done after all of the other exercises are complete, as they can get quite involved.

Here is a simple outline for a 90-120 minute group workshop. Each of the points below is an exercise in the book, listed in the Table Of Contents. This could work for any size group. With bigger groups, you will have participants break off into dyads or triads to do the work; for smaller groups, you can have more whole-group dialogue. When working with a bigger group, you can have anyone share anything with the big group that they heard or learned from the work in their small group (with consent!). You can adjust as needed for your time and audience. Consider that exercises usually take more time than expected.

Intro— Open with Land Acknowledgement and Ancestors Prayer

- Share the intention and flow of the time ahead. Read **Agreements**, invite any other agreements folx want to add and get a consensus.

1. **Binaries to Consider**—share list, ask for others, invite writing time and then small or full group shares on personal experiences. Dialogue depending on size of group and time
2. **Return to Beginner's Mind on Gender**—talk about what we have been conditioned to think gender is, what the current cultural norms are, what is changing, what has changed, and what people would like to see change.
3. **Mindfulness Meditation**—How's the Body?
4. **Dance Break!**—after deep talks, before folx get overdone - dance! Shake things up!
5. **Microaggressions**—introduce and reflect on the concept. Reflect on the questions in this section in the book and discuss. In dyads, do the **Exercise on Repair**

6. **Imagine If...** write & share about visions of what is possible for our world if we were to dispel binary thinking/ othering/ the illusion of separation

The content in this book has grown beyond the scope of one workshop, but being in reflection with the information and honestly investigating yourself through the prompts will give you the support you need to do this. Remember, it is best to invite people into reflection and self-investigation. Do not expect to *teach* anyone anything new or tell them how to think. Notice that most of the work we guided in this book was not about delivering facts for you to memorize or telling you how to be. We invited you in to various ways of seeing, investigating yourself, and relating to the world at large. How did that feel, what moved inside of you? This is the place you will best be ready to share from. We all learn best from direct experience. Doing the work proposed in this book creates direct experiences, especially when done with others.

I invite you to reach out to me and a community of beings who are working to dispel divisive binaries. Find further info and links to social media sites on the Dispelling the Binary page on my website @www.lucidyoga.com

HERE is the QR code to go to places to share your answers, add your stories and suggestions, and commune with others on this path of self-investigation and awakening into unity consciousness.

QR Code For Class Content
Ryoga Vee

Acknowledgements

After presenting much of this book's content in the summer of 2022, I got many requests to share the information for other folx to use with their communities. I wanted this information, the non-binary worldview, and practices to ripple out, so I was happy to oblige. I thought I would simply expand my notes for clarity and add helpful cues where necessary to help facilitators guide the experience. I figured that I would have that done in a few weeks since I had already had great support from Jess, Ola'i, turtle, and Jane's edits in prepping for the workshop. I was wrong. I kept getting new ideas about what was essential to add until it became a thick, chunky stew that I felt lost in. I didn't know where to stop following my inspirations! I talked to many folx about it as I worked and found others doing similar work. I learned about ALOK and their book "Beyond the Binary" as well as the book "Life Isn't Binary," which has a similar format and message in many parts. At that point, I almost gave up thinking these people had more cred, were queerer, more educated than me, and already had their work out in the world. I was too late, I thought. I recognize these thoughts now as the kinds of doubts that most creators have along the way to completion. What I also know to repeat to myself now, based on a gift that arose during meditation, is that WE CAN NEVER HAVE TOO MANY VOICES AMPLI-

FYING LOVE AND INSPIRATION! Only together can we create great waves of change! We must make the love revolution irresistible!

I asked Ola'i Wildeboar (aka Lali Wilde) to look at my expanded manuscript to see what they thought. She quickly saw how to move things around to make it more streamlined and digestible. I hired them instantly. We have continued to work together for the last two years while I've continued to present the content at workshops. With her brilliance for seeing the whole and organizing its parts and my continued learning through students and life, the work began to have its own life, guided by the patient support and brilliance of Ola'i. She held my hand through so many moments of stuckness. We emerged victorious.

Soon, it was ready to be test-printed and shared with others to get their feedback. Thank you to so many wonderful humans for taking the time to read and share feedback in this process: Jess Please, Eenor Wildeboar, Kathy Isbell, Peter Schurman, Arielle (Tonks) Tonkin (LOVE for ALL of it!), Stelle Bahrami, Ryoga Vee, aka the tool guy!, Renee Skarin, Kellie Nadler, Sweet Wild Rose, Rosy Moon, and Julie Feinstein. Thank you to Eve Isbell (&Tony & fam!) for a home away from home during some of the hardest times. Infinite love and gratitude to all of you, and special thanks to David Schlussel for following through with so many great suggestions and for your unwavering support in all areas of life as I continued to try to stay in the light without the light of our Jess love. Thank you, David Fore, for reading, your unwavering adhikara, and your generous heart of service with professional grief counseling through those crushing early weeks.

Infinite love and gratitude to the Chubb and Berkley family for your generous love and support through this past year as we all have dealt with the ultimate transition of our Jess love, and thank you for holding them with love and care through their gender transition as best as you could. Your love was always present and felt by them. I am so grateful to have you as family. Thank you for your continued care; I could not have completed this without it. Momma Pat, my heart is forever with you. Morris, Chris, Sarah, Gabe, Graham, Ana, and the extended family...We have an angel now.

Thank you to my beloved yogic communities for your empathy and support as I went through this process of healing and writing; your understanding was paramount to my well-being and the trust that I could pull back and care for myself and return to the fold of love and compassion at Green Yogi and Arise Yoga studios. Thank you, Naseim, Sonya, Maria Christina, Jillian, Jenny, Kathryn, Erika, all of the teachers who subbed for me, and all of the students who were there with us in the fullness of life and kept coming back. Deep pranams to the Yoga Teacher Training class of 2024, who received me broken open and equally witnessed how the practices are crucial to getting through the most challenging things in life. Our island was a refuge and forge for so much growth all around!

Thank you to Reverend Lien and Alejandra Siroka for your input on this project and dedication to supporting this kind of work in the world through your teachings.

Last but not least, when I asked Polly Superstar to read this, she directly challenged me with a big question. Did I want this work to be for the presenter or the participant in the workshop? Both, of course!, was my reply. But she made it clear that that didn't make for a clear presentation. So, I surrendered to her enthusiastic, insightful force of clarity. She did some incredible, what felt like "vacuuming" up of the bits inhibiting the messages in this work from being direct to the person doing the work. She became my line editor and helped me clear up my habitual words and incorrect use of dashes and dots. Thank you, Polly, for your keen insight and attention to so many things. You shined up this baby and helped us to birth it into the world, not too late at all. It is time.

About the Author

lucid dawn 2025 being nice
Hilary Nichols Photography

I am known as lucid dawn, my pronouns are she/they. I am a many-blooded, Turtle Island/United States-born being of the human race, a queer-identifying, pan-sexual, cis-femme human with non-binary leanings since childhood. I am a devoted Reclaiming witch & Tantrik yogi of non-dual Shakta-Shaiva lineages of Kashmir. My life's work and study has been about healing from trauma and discovering all that it is to be a whole human, free of shame, oppression, and the feelings of brokenness and not belonging that I grew up with. I acknowledge my privilege in being a non-disabled, pale-skinned female who can often "pass" (meaning get by without being noticed as different than expected) in homogenized environments when I feel the need to. My first and current loves are people of the in-between, trans folx. Many of my ancestors were Indigenous people who were silenced and taught to deny who they were, and that shame was passed down. All this and more has compelled me to be a voice for freedom of self-expression. It is my passionate dedication to be of service to the healing and awakening that is unfurling on our planet right now, for the well-being of our home planet itself, for my ancestors, and for those who will come after us.

lucid dawn is available to facilitate talks, community dialogue, workshops, lectures, courses, retreats, rituals, and themed connection events. Reach out to her @lucidyoga.com for inquiries and booking.

Glossary of Terms

ABRACADABRA!

From Aramaic, meaning "I create as I speak." Highlights the creative power of words and intentions in shaping reality.

Alchemical Marriage

A symbolic concept describing the union of opposites—such as masculine and feminine energies—often used to represent inner integration or wholeness.

Binary Thinking

The tendency to categorize concepts, ideas, or people into two opposing groups or options, such as "good vs. bad" or "male vs. female," often

oversimplifies complex realities and limiting perspectives.

Cognitive Dissonance

The psychological discomfort experienced when holding conflicting beliefs, values, or attitudes, often prompting a search for consistency.

Constructs

Socially or culturally created ideas or frameworks, such as race, gender, or class, that shape perceptions and influence behavior.

Dialectical Thinking

A mindset that embraces contradictions and seeks a synthesis between opposing ideas, fostering deeper understanding and resolution.

Dispelling

The act of breaking the power of a belief, concept, or construct by reframing, questioning, or releasing it. Derived from the Latin dispellere, meaning "to

drive apart."

Enantiodromia

A psychological principle where an extreme position or force naturally gives way to its opposite. Introduced by Heraclitus and later expanded by Carl Jung.

Gendersex, Gender/Sex

The concept of gendersex acknowledges the interconnectedness of sex and gender, recognizing that they both play a role in shaping an individual's identity and   experiences. While i didn't use this term in the book, it is becoming popularized, as in Augustin Fuentes' work, to use when it is not solely sex or gender facts

or influences that we are referring to.

Internal Family Systems (IFS)

A therapeutic framework that views the mind as composed of various "parts" (e.g., protectors,exiles) that interact with an inherent core "Self," focusing

on internal harmony and healing.

Intersectionality

A framework for understanding how overlapping social identities (e.g., race, gender, class) contribute to systemic oppression or privilege.

Liminal

Referring to in-between or transitional states, spaces, or experiences that are neither here nor there but hold potential for transformation.

Micro/Macrocosm

The principle that patterns or dynamics in smaller systems (micro) reflect those in larger

systems (macro), emphasizing interconnectedness.

Mycelial Network

A metaphor derived from fungi's interconnected root-like structures, symbolizing

interdependence and communication in natural and social systems.

Non-Duality

A philosophical or spiritual concept that suggests that apparent opposites (e.g., self/other, good/bad) are interconnected parts of a unified reality rather

than mutually exclusive. Non-duality *includes* perceived duality as an inherent part of the experience of being.

Non-Pathologizing

An approach to understanding behaviors, thoughts, or identities without labeling them as inherently disordered or abnormal.

"Purno'ham vimarsa"

A Sanskrit phrase meaning "I am full and complete," expressing the concept of inherent

wholeness in Tantrik philosophy.

Queer and Activist Ancestors

Historical figures who challenged societal norms and fought for equality often reclaim marginalized identities and inspire future generations.

Re-cognizing

A deliberate process of rethinking or seeing anew, especially to question inherited beliefs or constructs. Highlights the transformative act of gaining fresh

perspectives.

Re-membering

Bringing the members or parts of a whole (person, community, lineage) back into connection for healing and integration of what may have been

exiled, forgotten, or experienced as disparate parts.

Repression

The psychological suppression of impulses, memories, or desires that are perceived as unacceptable often leads to unconscious influences on behavior.

Sacred Masculine and Feminine

Archetypal energies representing traditional gender-associated traits are often used in spiritual contexts to explore balance and integration beyond

physical gender.

Sacred/Profane

A duality contrasts what is considered holy or spiritual (sacred) with what is deemed ordinary, taboo, or impure (profane).

Spectrums of Possibility

The idea that identities, experiences, or qualities exist on a continuum rather than as fixed, binary points allows for more nuanced understanding.

Spells of Separation

Metaphorical language referring to beliefs, constructs, or words that create division, fostering a sense of "othering" and disconnection.

Spiritual Bypass

The act of avoiding or repressing negative emotions or experiences by focusing solely on spiritual ideals or positive thinking.

Trauma Responses

Instinctive reactions to perceived danger are categorized as fight, flight, freeze, or fawn. These are survival mechanisms triggered by physical or emotional threats.

References & Resources

Sources used to compile worldwide gender variant names:
There was a lot of patching of information as there was no site with a complete list and some information differed, so there are not always direct quotes. Some of these resources also had in-depth stories of certain groups of folx and are worth looking more deeply into;

- https://www.bbc.com/travel/article/20210411-asias-isle-of-five-separate-genders
- https://www.bbc.com/travel/article/20181125-the-third-gender-of-southern-mexico
- https://www.theguardian.com/music/2010/oct/11/two-spirit-people-north-america
- From YES~! Magazine - June 2021https://www.yesmagazine.org/social-justice/2021/06/07/trans-history-gender-diversity
- https://nhm.org/stories/beyond-gender-indigenous-perspectives-muxe
- https://nhm.org/stories/beyond-gender-indigenous-perspectives-faafafine-and-faafatama
- https://nhm.org/stories/beyond-gender-indigenous-perspectives-mapuche

- *Source: Ana Mariella Bacigalupo Shamans of the Foye Tree: Gender, Power, and Healing among the Chilean Mapuche*
- *https://www.acluohio.org/en/news/transgender-people-have-always-existed*
- https://www.redeemer-cincy.org/uploads/images/gender-diversity-in-indigenous-cultures_205.pdf
- https://theanarchistlibrary.org/library/nsambu-za-suekama-my-gender-is-marronage
- https://ashleighshackelford.com/writing/2020/11/30/you-could-never-misgender-me
- https://lgbtqia.wiki/wiki
- https://adventuresintimeandgender.org/wormholes/world-genders/
- https://nmu.edu/gender/sites/gender/files/2021-01/Autumn%20Post%27s%20Cultural%20Analysis.pdf
- https://en.wikipedia.org/wiki/Two-spirit#:~:text=Two%2Dspirit%20(also%20known%20as,social%20role%20in%20their%20communities.
- https://theindigenist.wordpress.com/2014/09/07/two-spirit-term-in-north-american-tribal-languages/
- InstagramPost by DeColonize Myself made by Giiweden, w/research done by Kai Pyle, Manidoo Ma'iigan, and Charles Lippert

Scientific Studies & Publications on Sex & Gender

- https://www.scientificamerican.com/article/sex-redefined-the-idea-of-2-sexes-is-overly-simplistic1/

- *The Inclusion of Sex and Gender Beyond the Binary in Toxicology* - https://pmc.ncbi.nlm.nih.gov/articles/PMC9355551/
- *Only two sex forms but multiple gender variants: How to explain?* - https://pmc.ncbi.nlm.nih.gov/articles/PMC5824932/
- https://embryo.asu.edu/pages/biological-sex-and-gender-united-states
- *The Psychology of Sexual and Gender Diversity in the 21st Century: Social Technologies and Stories of Authenticity* - *https://psycnet.apa.org/fulltext/2024-85607-001.html*
- https://education.nationalgeographic.org/resource/how-science-is-helping-us-understand-gender/
- Williams Institute, UCLA School of Law. (2023). Mental health disparities among LGBTQ+ populations. Retrieved from https://williamsinstitute.law.ucla.edu
- Pew Research Center. (2022). Attitudes toward gender and sexuality. Retrieved from https://www.pewresearch.org
- *Sex Is a Spectrum, The Biological Limits of the Binary* - Augustin Fuentes, 2025

On GENDER & EQUALITY;

https://www.fordfoundation.org/news-and-stories/stories/posts/what-the-evolution-of-gender-can-teach-us-about-equality/

In April, 2014

India's Supreme Court has recognized transgender people as a third gender in a landmark ruling.

"It is the right of every human being to choose their gender," it said in granting rights to those who identify themselves as neither male nor female.

It ordered the government to provide transgender people with quotas in jobs and education in line with other minorities, as well as key amenities.

According to one estimate, India has about two million transgender people.

https://www.them.us/story/colonialism-black-and-indigenous-people-gender-identity

Inspirational Publications-On Living in the Liminal;

https://medium.com/@racheljones_698/betwixt-between-and-becoming-on-liminality-and-embracing-the-precarious-in-between-fce9d5aa3ef6

https://qz.com/1181019/the-japanese-words-for-space-could-change-your-view-of-the-world/

https://uwpress.wisc.edu/blog/?p=4337

https://nautil.us/at-home-in-the-liminal-world-1438/

https://www.ted.com/talks/jedidah_isler_the_untapped_genius_that_could_change_science_for_the_better/ transcript

https://onbeing.org/programs/john-odonohue-the-inner-landscape-of-beauty/

Science & Psychology References on Dialectical & Dichotomous Thinking;

https://www.psychologytoday.com/us/blog/she-comes-long-way-baby/201506/what-is-wrong-dichotomous-thinking

Dialectical Thinking - ScienceDirect - https://www.sciencedirect.com/science/article/abs/pii/S1077722922000438

Dialectical Thinking: A Proposed Foundation for a Postmodern Psychology - PMC - https://www.ncbi.nlm.nih.gov/pmc/articles/PMC9235839/

Dichotomous Thinking Leads to Entity Theories of Human Ability - https://files.eric.ed.gov/fulltext/ED535734.pdf

Queer & Trans Ancestor lists - https://borealisphilanthropy.org/2023/06/30/honoring-our-unapologetically-queer-and-trans-ancestors/

https://healthymindsphilly.org/blog/lgbtqia-ancestors/

On White Supremacy Culture (& how it feeds off of & perpetuates the binary) -

https://www.whitesupremacyculture.info/

Federal Reserve Report on Wealth Inequality (2019) https://www.federalreserve.gov/econres/notes/feds-notes/disparities-in-wealth-by-race-and-ethnicity-in-the- 2019-survey-of-consumer-finances-20200928.html

Resources for Information and Support for You:

Anti-Racism Resources:

- Anti-Racism Resource Library, AACP https://www.aacap.org/AACAP/Families_and_Youth/Resource_Libraries/Racism_Resource_Library.aspx
- Anti-Racism Resure List-Harvard School of Public Health https://www.hsph.harvard.edu/diversity/resources-training/harvard-chan-school/anti-racism-resource-list/

- National Equity Project https://www.nationale-quityproject.org/?gad_source=1

Gender & Sexuality Support Resources:

- Gender Spectrum- https://www.genderspectrum.org/
- LGBTQ Advocacy- GLAAD -https://glaad.org/
- LGBTQ Advocacy- PFLAG - https://pflag.org/
- The Trevor Project-24/7 Suicide Prevention & Crisis Intervention https://www.thetrevorproject.org/
- Human Rights Campaign, Equality for ALL- https://www.hrc.org/

Studies on Dualism & Binary Thinking:

https://www.nimh.nih.gov/health/statistics/major-depression
https://www.nami.org/about-mental-illness/mental-health-conditions/depression/
* https://pmc.ncbi.nlm.nih.gov/articles/PMC7819275/
National Alliance on Mental Illness (NAMI). (2023). The impact of mental health on binary thinking. Retrieved from https://nami.org
https://www.boyden.com/media/how-resilience-works/img/how-resilience-works.pdf

Related & Inspiring Books for further reference:

- *Transgender History, The Roots of Today's Revolution* by Susan Stryker
- *Feeding Your Demons* by Tsultrim Allione

- *Tantra Illuminated* by Christopher Hareesh Wallis
- *Indigenous Writes* by Chelsea Vowel
- *Changing Ones, Third and Fourth Genders in Native America* by Will Roscoe
- *Unseen Genders, Beyond the Binaries* by Lang, Haynes, McKenna
- *Two Spirit People, Native American Gender Identity, Sexuality, and Spirituality* by Jacobs, Thomas, & Lang
- *Gender Outlaw, On Men, Women & the Rest of Us* by Kate Bornstein
- *Hermaphrodeities, The Transgender Spirituality Workbook* by Raven Kaldera
- *Comfortable With Uncertainty* by Pema Chodron
- *Nobody Passes, Rejecting the Rules of Gender and Conformity* essays, edited by Matilda aka Matt Bernstein Sycamore
- *Beyond the Gender Binary* by Alok Vaid Menon
- *Life Isn't Binary* by Meg-John Barker & Alex Iantaffi
- *No Bad Parts* by Richard Schwartz
- *Queer Magic, Power Beyond Boundaries*-essays edited by Lee Harrington & Tai Fenix Kulystin
- *Caste, The Origins of Our Discontent* by Isabel Wilkerson
- *On Becoming a Person, A Therapists View of Psychotherapy* by Carl Rogers
- *The Body Keeps Score, Brain, Mind, and Body in the Healing of Trauma* by Bessel Van Der Kolk, MD
- *Waking the Tiger: Healing Trauma* by Peter A. Levine
- In An Unspoken Voice, How the Body Releases Trauma and Restores Goodness by Peter A. Levine
- *Dreaming the Dark, Magick, Sex & Politics* by Starhawk

- *The Collected Works of CG Jung, Volume 6, Psychological Types*
- *My Grandmothers Hands, Racialized Trauma and the Pathway to Mending Our Hearts and Bodies* by Resmaa Menakem
- *Evolution's Rainbow: Diversity, Gender, and Sexuality in Nature and People*, by Joan Roughgarden
- *Sex Is a Spectrum*, by Augustin Fuentes

Footnotes

1. Definitions from the Oxford English Language Online Dictionary ↑
2. in 2022, published in the journal Environmental Science & Technology Letters,https://pubs.acs.org/doi/full/10.1021/acs.estlett.2c00322, ↑
3. Mycelium video by National Geographic - https://fb.watch/vF4_rPPO3w/ ↑
4. **https://medium.com/sonderbodhi/the-theory-of-the-third-91925fe4ad06** ↑
5. From The Collected Works of CG Jung, references to enantiodromia appear throughout his works, but especially in Volume 6, *Psychological Types, &* Jung on Enantiodromia - https://jungiancenter.org/jung-on-the-enantiodromia-part-1-definitions-and-examples/ ↑
6. On Enantiodromia - with reference to Nietzsche and Heraclitus - https://en.wikipedia.org/wiki/Enantiodromia#:~:text=Jung%20was%20heavily%20influenced%20by,51). ↑
7. Internal Family Systems - a psychotherapeutic modality founded by Dick Schwartz. https://ifs-institute.com/. ↑
8. The Inclusion of Sex and Gender Beyond the Binary In Toxicology, National Institutes of Health article, @ https://pmc.ncbi.nlm.nih.gov/articles/PMC9355551 ↑

9. How Common Is Intersex? Article from the Intersex Society of North America https://isna.org/faq/frequency/ ↑

10. Article on Gender w/ reference to Margaret Mead's work, https://www.sagepub.com/sites/default/files/upm-binaries/101817_Ch11.pdf ↑

11. https://ictnews.org/archive/two-spirits-one-heart-five-genders, https://www.hrc.org/news/two-spirit-and-lgbtq-idenitites-today-and-centuries-ago ↑

12. The full resource list for this list is to be found in the back of the book in *the References* section ↑

13. burlesque noun: **burlesque**; plural noun: **burlesques** 1. an absurd or comically exaggerated imitation of something, especially in a literary or dramatic work; a parody. "the funniest burlesque of opera", humor that depends on comic imitation and exaggeration; absurdity.,"the argument descends into burlesque", 2. a variety show, typically including striptease.,"burlesque clubs".- From Oxford Languages Dictionary

14. From, The Yoga Sutras of Patanjali, translation & commentary by Chip Hartranft, Shambala Publishing ↑

15. Language Alchemy, founded by Alejandra Siroka - podcast, workshops, online course and private transformative communication coaching for multicultural change agents, couples, and groups seeking to create and maintain thriving, conscious relationships. https://www.languagealchemy.com/ . I highly recommend her and her work! ↑

16. Reverend Lien, **accesstozen.org** ↑

17. Articles & studies On Play as Therapy—https://www.ncbi.nlm.nih.gov/pmc/articles/PMC8812369/, https://www.brookings.edu/articles/learning-and-healing-through-play-in-humanitarian-crises/, https://www.thegoodtrade.com/features/how-to-be-playful/, https://nifplay.org/play-science/summary-of-key-findings/ ↑

YOU ARE BEAUTIFUL

YOU ARE LOVE